JOURNEY INTO THE HEART OF AUTHENTIC DISCIPLESHIP

THE DISCIPLESHIP

CHALLENGE

Written by Thomas E. Ward, Jr.

Cover Design by Keith Locke - CommuniGATOR

Cover images by Photodisc

Printed in the United States of America

TO MY PARENTS. THANK YOU FOR
FOLLOWING CHRIST AND LOVING GOD
WITH ALL OF YOUR HEART, SOUL, MIND,
AND STRENGTH.

TABLE OF CONTENTS

TABLE OF CONTENTS

DISCIPLEMAKING APPOINTMENTS

Next Meeting: **Time:**

Next Meeting: **Time:**

Next Meeting: **Time:**

Next Meeting: **Time:**

Next Meeting: **Time:**

Next Meeting: **Time:**

Next Meeting: **Time:**

Next Meeting: **Time:**

Next Meeting: **Time:**

Next Meeting: **Time:**

Next Meeting: **Time:**

Next Meeting: **Time:**

Next Meeting: **Time:**

Next Meeting: **Time:**

Next Meeting: **Time:**

DISCIPLEMAKING APPOINTMENTS

Next Meeting: **Time:**

Next Meeting: **Time:**

Next Meeting: **Time:**

Next Meeting: **Time:**

Next Meeting: **Time:**

Next Meeting: **Time:**

Next Meeting: **Time:**

Next Meeting: **Time:**

Next Meeting: **Time:**

Next Meeting: **Time:**

Next Meeting: **Time:**

Next Meeting: **Time:**

Next Meeting: **Time:**

WHAT IS THE DISCIPLESHIP CHALLENGE WORKBOOK?

The Discipleship Challenge Workbook is an investigative Bible study developed with the purpose of helping you become an authentic disciple of Jesus Christ. It is ideally suited for use in a one-on-one or small group setting, recognizing that spiritual growth cannot take place apart from continuous interaction with God's people. The entire manual, including each of the twenty-six sessions, is designed to help you cultivate the following:

> - A deeper relationship with God
> - A greater understanding of God's Word
> - A stronger connection with God's people
> - A lasting commitment to God's plan

These four objectives will begin to take shape in your life as you develop the three foundational disciplines of an authentic disciple:

> - Daily Interaction with God
> - Direct Involvement in the Local Church
> - Deliberate Investment in the Great Commission

As you begin to use this guide, along with your discipler or with a group of fellow disciples, the Word of God will come alive. You will soon realize that every aspect of your life is connected to what you believe about God, His Word, His people, and His plan for your life. You will be amazed as you uncover the rich treasures of the Bible, and begin to find yourself more eager to accomplish the kingdom agenda than anything else.

Remember, this is just the beginning of your lifelong journey to become an authentic disciple of Jesus Christ. You don't become a disciple when you arrive at a predetermined destination or finish a prescribed curriculum, but only when you are eagerly on the path with Christ, engaging in His work and accomplishing His mission.

HOW TO USE THIS WORKBOOK

This workbook has been written and designed for you to search, investigate, and discover the essential truths of the Christian faith as they are revealed in Scripture. One of the foremost goals in the entire discipleship process is to equip you to equip others. And there is no better way to become a reproducing leader than to become familiar with the only completely reliable disciplemaking manual—the Word of God. Every other discipleship resource, including this one, is flawed, because finite human beings have developed them. The Bible is the entirely trustworthy, fully inspired Word of God. Our intention throughout this workbook is to build your confidence in the absolute authority of God's Word. "How is this accomplished?" you might ask. It's accomplished most effectively through the following four strategies:

1. **Scripture memory**—built into each of the twenty-six sessions of this workbook is a memory verse that deals directly with that week's study. Every time you get together, you will be accountable to either your discipler or another small group member to have this verse memorized and ready to quote. Memorizing portions of Scripture is a mighty weapon in your spiritual arsenal.

2. **Scripture lookup**—because of the investigative nature of this manual, you will need a Bible and pen or pencil handy throughout your study. Each question is built around looking up a particular verse or series of verses in the Bible and answering the question related to those verses. This will allow you to become familiar with the structure and flow of God's Word.

3. **Scripture reading**—a key component of the discipleship process is to understand that your daily, personal relationship with God is the essential component of your spiritual growth. If you are not in God's Word, reading, studying, and delighting in its truths, then God will not be able to fully reveal Himself and His will to you. You are encouraged to make daily Bible reading a top priority.

4. **Scripture discussion**—one of the most exciting by-products of reading, studying, memorizing, and meditating on the Word of God is the opportunity to discuss what God has taught and revealed to you with another follower of Christ. Throughout this study, you will be encouraged and challenged to share your questions, comments, and experiences in God's Word with your discipler or within the safe environment of your small group.

OPTIMIZING THE DISCIPLEMAKING TIME

1

PRAY—In order to develop a balance between information and interaction, we would encourage regular and informal times of prayer and communication within the discipleship time. Prayer should not be thought of as the bookends for each meeting. There should be regular times of prayer scattered throughout each session. When you pray, you voluntarily recognize your complete dependence on God.

2

TALK—There should also be an ongoing dialogue about life. One of the greatest gifts of disciplemaking relationships is the ability to connect life experiences with Life himself—Jesus Christ. As one of His followers, you will soon recognize that a radical shift has taken place, and you now look to Christ, rather than yourself, as the center of everything. This fundamental change in your perspective develops as you engage in regular discussions with other followers of Christ about what is happening in your life.

3

PREPARE—While we would encourage you to experiment in your use of *The Discipleship Challenge Workbook*, weekly sessions are most effective when you work through the lesson in advance. Coming to your discipleship gathering inadequately prepared may lengthen the meeting and leave little or no time for discussion, prayer, and practical application.

WILL YOU TAKE THE DISCIPLESHIP CHALLENGE?

One of the most exciting adventure races in the world is the Eco-Challenge, a grueling three hundred mile event that touts itself as the toughest race on the planet. Each year, four-member teams converge at a pre-determined location to face off in what proves to be the ultimate battle of physical and mental endurance. As you might have already guessed, this is not a race for the faint of heart.

What sets the Eco-Challenge apart from every other competition like it is that each team member understands that for the next six to ten days he will sacrifice every conceivable comfort for the good of the team and for the chance to complete the exhausting trek. Just finishing the contest is a victory for even the most well trained team, because in order to finish the Challenge each member of the four-man squad must stay in the race or risk the entire group's disqualification. There are no injury "time outs" or excuses. In fact, many teams go days on end with little or no sleep. Why? The Eco-Challenge is a twenty-four hour a day race. From the moment you start the race until the time you complete the three hundred mile adventure, you are in a war against time, the other teams, and your collective ability to remain focused on the primary objective—the finish line.

For the past few years I have enjoyed watching the television shows that highlight this extraordinary event. My admiration for the intensity and drive of the competitors increases on an annual basis. I can tell, just by looking at each contestant's face, that this race is the toughest thing they have ever done. They are tired, muddy, scratched, bruised, scuffed, and usually soaking wet. I have often wondered, "What keeps them going? Why will these teams sacrifice everything to finish the race?" I certainly don't have all the answers to these questions, but I know that there are at least three things that motivate each of the participants—an incredible desire to reach beyond themselves, a powerful commitment to their team's overall success, and an uncommon sense of purpose.

Now, let's talk about discipleship. Are you beginning to see some very strong similarities between the Eco-Challenge and The Discipleship Challenge? Friends, we are in a race. We are in a battle. We are running in a spiritual marathon with very serious consequences for those who are unable to finish well. Just like the Eco-Challenge, the discipleship process is not a journey for the faint of heart. Life-on-life discipleship will cost you something. It will require personal sacrifice. And above all, it is a group effort. When one person bails out or comes up lame, it costs the whole team. Your spiritual growth is never self-achieved. It is, in large part, the result of your lifelong interaction with those who also belong to Jesus Christ.

How ironic that almost two thousand years after Jesus issued His final command to go and make disciples we would find ourselves admiring the intensity and drive of a group of athletes as they compete in one of the most difficult races in the world. This workbook is actually a proposal to recover what we've lost since the days of the early church, when nonbelievers looked to Christians to find lasting commitment, total surrender, self-sacrifice, and a bold mission to help people become authentic disciples of Jesus Christ.

No matter what the cost, let's begin to reclaim the rich legacy of disciplemaking that permeated church life nearly two thousand years ago. And while others look to athletes and competitions to find their inspiration, may God look down from Heaven and find His joy in our renewed efforts to take The Discipleship Challenge seriously.

WHAT IS AN AUTHENTIC DISCIPLE?

When we talk about the qualities of an authentic disciple, remember that we are always talking about the ideal, understanding that our humanity will always undermine our most noble efforts to follow Christ. Until heaven, we will never be perfect, but until heaven we must always strive to be like Someone who is. "An unattainable goal," you might say. True. But should that stop us from attempting, through the power of the Holy Spirit, to be like Christ? Think about it. What baseball pitcher who threw thirteen strikeouts wasn't trying to strike out every batter he faced? What Christian employer who lost his temper a few times with his employees wasn't attempting to keep his composure at all times? What craftsman worth his salt isn't endeavoring to build the perfect house every time he picks up a hammer and nails? Becoming more like Jesus is a daily pursuit that lasts for an entire lifetime. It doesn't just happen. It is happening. Recognizing the difference will prevent you from becoming frustrated and defeated in the process.

SIX CHARACTERISTICS OF AN AUTHENTIC DISCIPLE

The following characteristics of authentic disciples are centered on principles, not performance standards or well-defined lists of do's and don'ts. Each one represents a fundamental quality that Jesus was attempting to forge into the lives of His first disciples. As you review these traits, it would be especially helpful to read the corresponding Scripture given with each characteristic. This will allow you to experience the heart and mind of the Master, as He casts His vision for what should typify the life of an authentic disciple.

Authentic disciples live according to the teachings, insights, values, and commandments of Jesus Christ, always recognizing the counter-cultural nature of their new and unique life calling as citizens of God's eternal Kingdom (Luke 5:1-11; 27-39; 6:20-49; 22:24-30).

Authentic disciples value the advancement of God's Kingdom over any other human agenda, continually placing the cause of Christ far above their own self-interests and personal ambitions (Luke 5:27-39; 9:18-27; 57-62; 10:1-24).

Authentic disciples allow God to be God, constantly relying on Him for physical and spiritual nourishment; forgiveness and the power to forgive; leadership and strength to complete their life's mission (Luke 11:1-13).

Authentic disciples strive for integrity in every area of their lives, faithfully demonstrating the wisdom and discernment to manage all of their God-given resources and relationships with excellence (Luke 12:1-12; 16:1-13; 17:1-10).

Authentic disciples live with a sense of vision and hope for the future, confidently awaiting their Leader's return while aggressively keeping His Great Commission their primary passion (Luke 21:5-36).

Authentic disciples treasure the power and presence of the Holy Spirit in their lives, joyfully accepting His role as Counselor, Comforter, Teacher, and Guide (Luke 24:44-49).

WHAT IS DISCIPLESHIP?

Throughout the New Testament, discipleship emerges as the primary catalyst for spiritual formation. Jesus Christ modeled a lifestyle of both *witness* and *withness* (Mark 3:14). He knew that in order for His mission to continue after He was gone, He would have to proclaim the Good News. But Jesus was even more keenly aware of His responsibility to be with a group of eager learners, mentoring, motivating, and mobilizing a small army of Kingdom-minded soldiers to continue the all-important task of making disciples. After all, the future of the Church depended on their complete and total understanding of the disciple-making process.

Christ knew, and He wanted His disciples to know, that spiritual reproduction would never take place if making disciples was regarded as a low priority item on the early Church's to-do list. And just in case the disciples had plans to replace the Church's primary mission with another less important activity, Jesus once again reiterated the objective when He left them and us with His disciplemaking manifesto—the Great Commission (Matthew 28:18-20).

But perhaps most obvious about the disciplemaking style of Jesus is the noticeable lack of a prescribed curriculum. Apparently, Jesus was making a point that wherever disciplemaking efforts are going to flourish a workbook would not be in the foreground. Jesus' unstated goal in discipleship was to complete the person, not the curriculum. He was far more concerned with people, than He was with programs. Spiritual maturity was at the center of His disciplemaking strategy. Materials were secondary.

Always keep in mind that workbooks like this one and others merely serve as supplements to the help given by the Word of God, the Spirit of God, and the people of God. When completing the material takes priority over completing the person, needs go unmet; hearts are left unchanged; and unhealthy disciplemaking patterns emerge that will impact future generations of disciples.

The heart of discipleship is based on an interactive relationship with Jesus Christ. It focuses on a profound commitment to the Master, not just a passive conversion. During His earthly ministry, Jesus knew that in order to distinguish the spectators from the players He would have to make some demands that would begin to separate His true followers from those who were just along for the ride. Christ had no time for half-hearted devotion. As far as He was concerned, it was all or nothing. His greatest passion was to turn eager learners into reproducing leaders that He could personally entrust with His disciplemaking mission.

Christ wants all of you. Ninety-five percent is not enough. Ninety-nine percent still falls short. What are you holding back from Christ? What do you still have in your grasp that keeps you from living a life that is fully devoted to Him? He has sacrificed everything, including His life, so that you might experience all the fullness and joy of living as one of His followers.

> "DISCIPLESHIP BEGINS WHEN YOU FULLY RELINQUISH ALL THAT SEPARATES YOU FROM JESUS CHRIST."

Discipleship begins when you fully relinquish all that separates you from Jesus Christ. Therefore, authentic, biblical discipleship is the ongoing process of developing a lifelong, obedient relationship with Jesus Christ in which He:

- lovingly restores your broken relationship with God,
- supernaturally indwells you with His promised Holy Spirit,
- graciously connects you with others who follow Him,
- radically transforms your character and values,
- eagerly involves you in His disciplemaking mission.

WHAT DOES THE DISCIPLEMAKING PROCESS LOOK LIKE?

Disciplemaking is the work that Jesus Christ has entrusted His Church to accomplish (Matthew 28:18-20; 1 Corinthians 15:58). It encompasses the four-fold responsibility of every Christ follower to evangelize, establish, edify, and equip people to finish the task that Jesus Christ began during His earthly ministry (John 17:1-18). Jesus Christ made it crystal clear that disciplemaking is the responsibility of every child of God, and that in order for Him to return, the gospel would first have to be proclaimed to the entire world (Matthew 24:14). Christ's job is to obediently return for the Church when His Father gives the go ahead. In the meantime, our job is to obediently offer ourselves as servants of the Great Commission—to fulfill Jesus' final command with all of the strength we can muster.

PAINTING THE DISCIPLEMAKING PICTURE

At the center of all of our disciplemaking efforts is God. Without Him our most well conceived strategies and plans for making disciples would fail. We cannot and should not enter into any disciplemaking union, whether as a discipler or disciple, unless we have fully surrendered the entire process to God. As mentioned earlier, curriculum does not complete a person; God does.

Ultimately, it is God, through His Word and His Spirit, who brings salvation, stability, support, and strength to every disciple. Fortunately, He uses us as His instruments in evangelizing, establishing, edifying, and equipping people to become reproducing leaders for the furtherance of His kingdom. Just to be included in this worldwide redemptive drama should fill our hearts with joy. The God of heaven has chosen to use us as His catalytic change agents in the hearts and lives of all who would believe in His Son.

God knew the significance that caring, disciplemaking relationships would have on the entire spiritual development process of a new disciple. If you are a parent or close to someone who is, consider the maturing process of a human being. When a new life enters the world, this infant demands the attention of a capable adult—someone who is able to protect her, feed her, wash her, dress her, and meet every conceivable need that she may express through her crying and tears. And until the day when the child can adequately care for herself, a provider-parent is always present. The goal is to invest ample amounts of love, time, energy, and training into the life of the child, so that one day she will flourish in adulthood.

Spiritually speaking, the parenting metaphor is very significant (1 Thessalonians 2:1-11). New spiritual life requires constant care from spiritual parents. Jesus' own investment of three years into the lives of His disciples is the earliest New Testament example of a Father nurturing His spiritual children. His commitment to their growth was absolute and unfailing. In fact, His parenting continued through the permanent indwelling of the Holy Spirit. If new Christians do not have undivided spiritual care provided by compassionate spiritual parents, they will shrivel up and die in their development.

Throughout the growth process, from birth to adulthood, the child learns, labors, and will eventually lead his own children. The greatest joy for any parent is to become a grandparent. When new life enters the world through the process of reproduction, the family is expanded, life is celebrated, and love is expressed in a myriad of ways. This should also be true within the family of God. Spiritual reproduction should be taking place all of the time as a normal function of disciplemaking relationships. Spiritual parents should be celebrating the births of their spiritual grandchildren on a continual basis.

In order to help you fully understand the disciplemaking process, a diagram has been created to assist you in visualizing your own spiritual development. It is conveniently arranged in the shape of a baseball diamond. However, our intention is not to encourage you to think that once you have reached home plate as a reproducing leader, you have arrived as an authentic disciple. In fact, just the opposite is true. We want you to understand that once you have made it to home plate, you are just beginning the most significant phase of your discipleship challenge—spiritual reproduction. Without question, this will be the most rewarding part of your discipleship journey.

THE DISCIPLEMAKING PROCESS

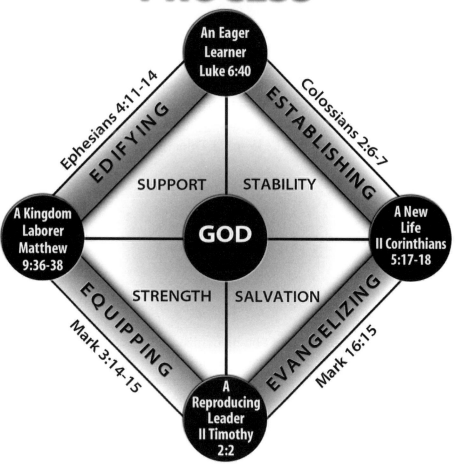

An Eager Learner
Luke 6:40

Ephesians 4:11-14

EDIFYING

Colossians 2:6-7

ESTABLISHING

SUPPORT   STABILITY

A Kingdom
Laborer
Matthew
9:36-38

GOD

A New
Life
II Corinthians
5:17-18

STRENGTH   SALVATION

EQUIPPING

Mark 3:14-15

EVANGELIZING

Mark 16:15

A
Reproducing
Leader
II Timothy
2:2

INTRODUCTION

Why are the three foundational disciplines of an authentic disciple such an essential part of the spiritual growth process? How would you evaluate the implementation of these key disciplines in your life right now? *(The back of this workbook (Appendix A) contains a discipleship inventory that may help you answer this question more accurately.)*

Why should the Word of God have such a significant place in the disciplemaking process? In what ways has the Bible helped you grow spiritually? Do you think a new Christian can grow apart from the truth of God's Word (1 Peter 2:2-3)?

What are a few of the similarities that you recognized between the Eco-Challenge and disciplemaking? Do you think the author paints an unrealistic picture of the discipleship process by using this analogy? Why or why not? (Consider the Apostle Paul's intensity in the following verses: Colossians 1:9-10; 28-29; Philippians 4:9; 1 Thessalonians 2:17-20; Galatians 4:19; Colossians 2:6-7.)

Why do you think the author spends such a great deal of time stressing the fact that discipleship and disciplemaking is a process? Has this changed your view of what becoming an authentic disciple is really all about? How?

Did you find yourself trying to "measure up" to the six characteristics of an authentic disciple? Why do you think we, as human beings and even as disciples, have a natural tendency to compare ourselves and others to the ideal? Is it unrealistic to think that we'll ever reach perfection as a follower of Christ? Why? How are these traits different than a man-made list of do's and don'ts?

Do you agree with the author's claim that true discipleship is always centered on your life in Christ? Why or why not? In one sentence or less, how would you describe discipleship?

What "base" are you currently at or approaching in the disciplemaking process? Do you understand the importance of moving around the diamond and becoming a reproducing leader? Explain.

THE DISCIPLESHIP CHALLENGE
COVENANT

I will strive to make attendance at all disciplemaking sessions a top priority.

I will strive to incorporate, with God's help, the following six characteristics of an authentic disciple into my life:

- Authentic disciples live according to the teachings, insights, values, and commandments of Jesus Christ, always recognizing the counter-cultural nature of their new and unique life calling as citizens of God's eternal Kingdom (Luke 5:1-11; 27-39; 6:20-49; 22:24-30).

- Authentic disciples value the advancement of God's Kingdom over any other human agenda, continually placing the cause of Christ far above their own self-interests and personal ambitions (Luke 5:27-39; 9:18-27; 57-62; 10:1-24).

- Authentic disciples allow God to be God, constantly relying on Him for physical and spiritual nourishment; forgiveness and the power to forgive; leadership and strength to complete their life's mission (Luke 11:1-13).

- Authentic disciples strive for integrity in every area of their lives, faithfully demonstrating the wisdom and discernment to manage all of their God-given resources and relationships with excellence (Luke 12:1-12; 16:1-13; 17:1-10).

- Authentic disciples live with a sense of vision and hope for the future, confidently awaiting their Leader's return while aggressively keeping His Great Commission their primary passion (Luke 21:5-36).

- Authentic disciples treasure the power and presence of the Holy Spirit in their lives, joyfully accepting His role as Counselor, Comforter, Teacher, and Guide (Luke 24:44-49).

I will strive to make the following three disciplines a vital part of my life as a follower of Jesus Christ:

- Daily Interaction with God

- Direct Involvement in the Local Church

- Deliberate Investment in the Great Commission

Signed: _____ Date: _____

THE BIBLE: ESTABLISHING A FOUNDATION FOR LIFE

INTRODUCTION

What is the final authority in your life? Where do you turn when everything around you seems to be turned upside down? When the reality of life hits you right between the eyes, and you are forced to face it, what do you find yourself leaning on?

Hold on! Before you answer prematurely, take a moment to think about it. How do you determine your moral and spiritual values? What points you to true north on your ethical compass? How do you find the distant shore in a windswept sea of fear and frustration? I know what you must be thinking—too many questions. But for just a moment consider the life you have already been allowed to live; whether your life has been good or bad is not the issue. The important thing is to carefully reflect upon what foundation your life has been built. Who was the builder and what materials were used?

Okay, now imagine that you are getting a fresh start. And no matter how weak and poorly built your first foundation was, you are getting a second chance to lay a brand new foundation—a sure foundation. May I suggest that the most rock-solid absolutely reliable foundation in the world is the Bible. Building your life on the Scriptures is by far the most worry-free way to go. You never have to be concerned about the credibility of the Builder, because the Builder of the life you've always wanted is God, and the foundation of that life is His Word.

SESSION ONE

UNDERSTANDING THE BIBLE

Memory Verse: Hebrews 4:12

WHAT IS THE WORD OF GOD?

How do you begin to understand a book like the Bible? A quick overview will at least provide you with a framework from which to begin to build your understanding. Here are a few of the really important facts about the Bible:

- The Bible is a library of 66 individual books, beginning with Genesis and ending with Revelation. (The word *Bible* actually means "the Book.")
- The Bible took over 1,500 years to produce.

- The Bible was written by 40 different authors.
- The Bible unfolds God's redemptive purpose and plan for humanity.
- The Bible has five recurring themes:

  1. The character of the triune God (Malachi 3:6)
  2. The penalty for sin and disobedience (Romans 6:23)
  3. The eternal rewards for faith and obedience (Ephesians 2:8-9)
  4. The Son of God and His sacrifice for sin (John 3:16)
  5. The second coming of Jesus Christ (2 Peter 3:14)

Now that you have seen these facts about the Word of God, list one or two of your questions or comments:

As you deepen your understanding of the Bible, it is very important to know the structural makeup of the Bible itself. The Word of God is composed of two Testaments, the Old and the New. (The word *Testament* actually means "covenant" or "agreement.") Each Testament shares equal significance and tells the continuing story of God's redemptive purpose and plan for humanity.

THE OLD TESTAMENT

The first major division of the Bible, the Old Testament, tells us the story of the creation of the universe and ends about four hundred years before the birth of Jesus Christ. Below are a few highlights:

- The Old Testament has 39 individual books (beginning with Genesis and ending with Malachi).
- The Old Testament has 3 different kinds of books:

  1. History books (17 books)
  2. Poetry books (5 books)
  3. Prophecy books (17 books)

- The Old Testament majors on the history of Israel and the promise of the coming Messiah.
- Upon completion of the Old Testament, there were 400 years of silence during which God did not inspire any Scripture. (The word *Scripture* or *Scriptures* actually means "sacred writings.")

THE OLD TESTAMENT AT A GLANCE

HISTORY	POETRY	PROPHECY
Genesis	Job	Isaiah
Exodus	Psalms	Jeremiah
Leviticus	Proverbs	Lamentations
Numbers	Ecclesiastes	Ezekiel
Deuteronomy	Song of Solomon	Daniel
Joshua		Hosea
Judges		Joel
Ruth		Amos
1 Samuel		Obadiah
2 Samuel		Jonah
1 Kings		Micah
2 Kings		Nahum
1 Chronicles		Habakkuk
2 Chronicles		Zephaniah
Ezra		Haggai
Nehemiah		Zechariah
Esther		Malachi

THE NEW TESTAMENT

The second major division of the Bible is the New Testament. The New Testament records the story from the birth of Christ to the culmination of all of history. A few of the highlights are listed below:

- The New Testament has 27 individual books (beginning with Matthew and ending with Revelation).
- The New Testament has 3 different kinds of books:

    1. History books (5 books)
    2. Teaching books (21 books)
    3. Prophecy books (1 book)

- The New Testament centers on the person of Christ and the establishment of His church.

THE NEW TESTAMENT AT A GLANCE

HISTORY	TEACHING	PROPHECY
Matthew	Romans	Revelation
Mark	1 Corinthians	
Luke	2 Corinthians	
John	Galatians	
Acts	Ephesians	
	Philippians	
	Colossians	
	1 Thessalonians	
	2 Thessalonians	
	1 Timothy	
	2 Timothy	
	Titus	
	Philemon	
	Hebrews	
	James	
	1 Peter	
	2 Peter	
	1 John	
	2 John	
	3 John	
	Jude	

The significance and importance of the Bible to impact your life should never be underestimated. But the Word of God, like anything in life that is worth loving and appreciating, must be something that you are familiar with, that you believe in, and that you are ready to apply to your life. God has given you a wonderful resource and treasure chest of practical application in His Word.

What seven words does the Psalmist use to describe the Word of God in Psalm 19:7-9? What four benefits are derived from God's Word (verses 7-8)?

WHY WAS THE WORD OF GOD WRITTEN?

The most popular book of all time is the Bible. It has been read by more people and published in more languages than any other book. Throughout history it has stood innumerable assaults from cultural, political, and even religious leaders. Yet in the end, it continues its worldwide dominance as the most important piece of literature ever recorded and reproduced for people to read. It is the very words of God, and it was written as a guidebook for your life—a divinely inspired instruction manual.

THE FOUR PURPOSES OF THE BIBLE

1. To reveal the triune God to people

The Bible is God's self-revelation. Throughout the Word of God He has chosen to reveal Himself to people through various means.

In the Old Testament He revealed Himself through:

- Creation—man, who is made in the image of God (Genesis 1:27)
- Angels (Genesis 18:1-3; Exodus 3:2)
- Signs, wonders, and miracles (Exodus 10:1-2)
- Visions and dreams (Isaiah 6:1-5)
- The spoken word of prophets and others (Jeremiah 1:9-10)
- The Old Testament writings

And in the New Testament He revealed Himself through:

- Creation—Jesus Christ, who is the very image of God (Colossians 1:15)
- Angels (Luke 1:26-33)
- Signs, wonders, and miracles (Luke 7:10-17)
- Visions and dreams (Acts 9:1-6)
- The spoken word of apostles and others (Acts 2:14-17)
- The indwelling Holy Spirit (Acts 1:8; 2:38)
- The New Testament writings

Read Isaiah 40:8. According to this verse, how long will the Word of God endure? Do you really believe this is true? Explain.

2. To teach people how to live

Not only is the Bible God's self-revelation, but it is also life's survival guidebook. It teaches you how to live with a total and complete dependence on God and His Word. In the Bible you find a sense of direction and purpose. In the Bible you find inspiring stories of hope and survival that empower you to continue on in the journey. And in the Bible you are reminded of the compassion of a loving God who taught the greatest lesson of surrender and sacrifice that you will ever know through His Son Jesus Christ (John 3:16).

According to Romans 15:4, why was the Bible written? And what do the Scriptures give you according to this verse?

Read 2 Timothy 3:16-17. What four things do these verses tell you that the Word of God is useful or profitable for?

3. To show God interacting with people

All throughout history God has been in constant contact with the human race. From Adam and Eve in the Garden to the three Hebrew children in the fiery furnace, God the Creator has chosen to interact with the people He has created. He has revealed Himself to us through His Word. He teaches us and guides us throughout the pages of Scripture, and He interacts with us through His Holy Spirit, as well as through other revelations that are recorded in the Bible. He is a God of interaction and connection to a group of people that He longs to be in relationship with.

Read the following accounts of God interacting with people:

- Enoch—Genesis 5:23-24
- Abram—Genesis 12:1-3
- Shadrach, Meshach, and Abednego—Daniel 3
- Saul—Acts 9:1-9
- Peter—Acts 10:9-23

What other biblical accounts can you recall where God interacted with people?

In Hebrews 1:1 you find that God interacted with people in other ways. According to this verse, in what way do you find God speaking to people in the past?

4. To show people the way back to God

One of the most important purposes of Scripture is to bring people back to God. The redemptive story that unfolds throughout the Bible's pages is a constant reminder that God desires to be in relationship with people. He is not some cosmic force who has chosen to leave behind His creation. But instead, God chose to reveal Himself through His Son Jesus Christ so that all men who receive the Son might be reconciled to the Father. The Bible, from Genesis to Revelation, is a record of people being shown the way back to God, followed by God's gracious and loving acceptance back into that eternal relationship that He originally intended (John 14:6).

DISCUSSION QUESTIONS

SESSION ONE

Who is the person in your life that you turn to when everything around you seems to be turned upside down? What makes you so dependent on this person?

Why do you think the Bible should be the book you turn to when everything in your life is crazy or calm? Who is revealed in the Bible?

What story unfolds throughout the pages of the Bible? How has this story intersected with your life?

What does the word *Bible* actually mean? What does the word *testament* actually mean? What does the word *Scripture* actually mean? What do these definitions reveal to you about the Word of God?

What are the four purposes of the Bible? What significance do these four purposes have in our daily lives?

Why is it so important for the Bible to show God interacting with the human race? What does this truth reveal to us about God?

What is one thing about the Bible that you learned as a result of studying this lesson?

TRUSTING THE BIBLE

Memory Verse: 2 Timothy 3:16-17

IS THE WORD OF GOD RELIABLE?

When we begin to think of the Bible's reliability, we are drawn to Paul's second letter to Timothy, specifically, 2 Timothy 3:16, where it speaks of Scripture being inspired or literally—"God-breathed." This is a startling truth that all of Scripture, every writing of God, has been "breathed out" by God. Therefore, all Scripture is inspired because it has been miraculously "God-breathed." That is inspiration.

Now we can begin to understand that "*revelation* occurred when God gave His truth. *Inspiration* occurred when the writers of Scripture received and recorded His truth. Today, when we understand and apply His truth, that's *illumination*."[1] You should make every effort to know the three terms just given above as well as the corresponding meaning. These key words will be referred to again and again throughout your Christian walk.

Based on what you just read, define the following words:

• Inspiration:

• Revelation:

• Illumination:

As a Christian, you can "affirm the infallibility and inerrancy of the Bible...because God is incapable of inspiring falsehood, His word is altogether true and trustworthy."[2] The Bible that you hold in your hand, inspired by God and communicated through the Holy Spirit to human writers, cannot contain errors based on the nature and character of its source—God. That means that you can be completely confident that the Word of God that you rely and depend on is true and trustworthy. It cannot lead you down the wrong path or in the wrong way. Its very words are life.

There are also clear benefits of relying on the Bible. We find these benefits in Psalm 119:98-100. Read this short passage and then answer the following questions:

• In Psalm 119:98, what is the first benefit of relying on the Bible?

• Verse 99 records a second benefit of relying on the Bible. What is it?

• Finally, in verse 100 we find a third benefit of relying on the Bible. What is it?

What questions or doubts do you have as you begin to understand and trust in the reliability of the Word of God?

WHAT DOES THE WORD OF GOD SAY ABOUT ITSELF?

The Old Testament writers claim to be writing or speaking God's words over 2,600 times. And then when you arrive in the New Testament, you find the writers referring back to these men on many different occasions (2 Peter 1:19-21). Jesus alone quoted from over 22 Old Testament books during His time on earth. In fact, Jesus was the fulfillment of many Old Testament prophecies concerning the coming Messiah. Consider the following prophecies and their corresponding fulfillment:

OLD TESTAMENT PROPHECIES FULFILLED

TOPIC	O.T. PROPHECY	N.T. FULFILLMENT
Jesus' Place of Birth	Micah 5:2	Matthew 2:1
Jesus' Virgin Birth	Isaiah 7:14	Matthew 1:18
Jesus' Triumphal Entry	Zechariah 9:9	John 12:13-14
Jesus' Betrayal	Psalm 41:9	Mark 14:10
Jesus' Rejection	Isaiah 53:3	John 1:11
Jesus' Crucifixion	Isaiah 53:12	Matthew 27:38
Jesus' Resurrection	Psalm 16:10	Acts 3:15
Jesus' Ascension	Psalm 68:18	Acts 1:9

What do the following authors in Scripture say about the source of their words?

Joshua—Joshua 1:1:

Jeremiah—Jeremiah 1:1-2:

David—2 Samuel 23:2:

Ezekiel—Ezekiel 1:2-3:

Isaiah—Isaiah 43:1:

Paul—I Corinthians 11:23:

According to Mark 12:24, what happens as a result of not knowing the Scriptures?

To what is the Word of God compared in the following verses?

• **Jeremiah 23:29:**

• **Matthew 4:4:**

• **Hebrews 4:12:**

• **James 1:23-25:**

What words does the writer of Hebrews use to describe Scripture (Hebrews 4:12)? Which one is the most significant to you?

What did the Psalmist say about the truth of God's Word in Psalm 119:160?

WHAT ABOUT THE WORK OF THE HOLY SPIRIT?

Certainly the witness of the writers and the fulfillment of the prophecies concerning Jesus give you ample evidence that the Bible is the inspired Word of God, but what about the work and influence of the Holy Spirit? You can be sure that believing that the Bible is the perfect Word of God is not simply an intellectual decision, but it is an evidence of the influence of the Holy Spirit on your life (John 14:26). In other words, you will not believe the Bible until the Holy Spirit has done His work of convincing you.

Part of the Holy Spirit's work is to reveal God to you, and this is done primarily through God's Word. Remember, you will never be convinced of the Bible's ultimate authority and validity apart from the Holy Spirit.

The Apostle Paul understood the importance of the Holy Spirit in convincing us that the Bible is the inspired Word of God. In his first letter to the Corinthians he talks about the Holy Spirit's critical work in revealing God to us. Read I Corinthians 2:9-16 and then answer the following questions taken from Paul's letter:

• According to this passage, how is God revealed to us (vss. 10-12)?

• Who knows the thoughts of God according to verse 11?

• Can non-Christians understand the things of God according to verse 14?

• According to verse 16, you have the mind of _____.

The Holy Spirit is the final witness for the proof of the Bible's authority and validity. You can now begin to understand what Paul was talking about in I Corinthians 1:21 when he said that people who don't accept the truth of God and His Word consider the preaching of the Cross foolishness. It is foolish to them because they are unable to receive the things of God (I Corinthians 2:14).

So you must allow the Holy Spirit to do His work of convincing you and influencing you that the Bible is the inspired Word of God, while at the same time praying for Him to work in the lives of those without Christ, the spiritually lost. Your greatest desire should be for the entire world to share in the message of the Gospel and the truth of God's inspired Word.

Have you allowed the Holy Spirit to do His work of convincing you that the Bible is the inspired Word of God? If not, ask God right now to send the Holy Spirit to touch your heart with this powerful truth.

DISCUSSION QUESTIONS

SESSION TWO

Why is it so important for Christians to believe in the inspiration of the Bible? What does the word *inspiration* mean?

What are the main differences between inspiration, revelation, and illumination? Which member of the Godhead is responsible for illuminating the Scriptures?

Why can't the Bible ever lead you down the wrong path or in the wrong way? To what extent should we allow the truth of God's Word to guide us then?

How many times did the Old Testament writers claim to be speaking or writing God's words? Why is this significant?

List several practical reasons why Jesus would refer to the Old Testament writings so often.

Is there any Scriptural evidence to support the claim that a person can believe the Bible is the inspired Word of God apart from the work of the Holy Spirit? Can it be solely an intellectual decision? Why not?

In what way has your confidence in the reliability and authenticity of God's Word been increased as result of this study?

THE WORD OF GOD GIVES SPIRITUAL LIFE

3

Memory Verse: 1 Peter 1:23

If you were to take the world's greatest work of art and place it in a favorite spot in your kitchen or living room, do you think that over time it would have the power to change your life? If you stared at it long enough, would you become a different person? Hopefully, you have already answered that question in your mind. The answer is an emphatic "No!" While the art may inspire you in your own artistic pursuits, it has no power or authority to change you. But if you were to give the Bible a significant place in your life, and you were to begin reading its pages and learning and applying its truths, it would radically transform you. While the artwork is inanimate and contains no life, the Bible is alive and full of incredible amounts of life-changing application.

The Bible's significance comes not just from the fact that it is the most popular book of all time. But even more importantly, its significance is derived exclusively from its source—God. God has left you His words in book form. His message that is to be read and adored is found in the Bible. The Bible is the only book that can transform you from the inside out, but you have got to give the Bible a place of priority in your life.

What amount of time do you currently give each day to reading and studying the Word of God? Based on your answer, can you honestly say that the Bible has a place of priority in your life?

One of the most amazing truths in the Bible is that the Word of God was active in your salvation. In fact, the Word of God is one of the agents that brings about the new birth. When you are born again, you are given a new beginning, a new life. Theologians refer to this new birth as regeneration. "Regeneration is the work of the Holy Spirit upon those who are spiritually dead (see Ephesians 2:1-10)."[3] When you were saved, you become a totally new creation. "In regeneration, God plants a desire for Himself in the human heart that otherwise would not be there."[4] This "desire" is manifested through an increased passion for spiritual things—things not of this world. The Word of God plays a pivotal role in the process of regeneration.

Read 1 Peter 1:23 and then answer the following questions:

• What does the phrase "born again" mean? Is this a physical rebirth?

• What type of seed are you born of? What do you think the word "seed" refers to?

• How were you born again according to this verse?

According to James 1:21, what can save you?

In Paul's summary of the Gospel in I Corinthians 15:1-4, he points out that the Gospel message that he preached came "according to the Scriptures." What three themes did Paul's Gospel contain?

1.

2.

3.

As you begin to understand the role of the Bible in your salvation, you begin to appreciate with a new sense of wonder the Word of God's incredible impact on your life, as well as marvel at its impact on the millions that have gone before you. Because Scripture instructs you for salvation, It instructs you about Christ. The reason you love the Bible is because it tells you about Christ. The Bible is God's canvas, upon which Christ's portrait has been beautifully painted for the whole world to enjoy.

In 2 Timothy 3:15, Paul is encouraging and reminding Timothy of the power of the Scriptures. The same Scriptures that Timothy had been taught as a child (verse 15) and learned more about as an adult (verse 14) were still able to alter the course of life for anyone that would believe in them. Read 2 Timothy 3:15 and take a moment to answer the questions below.

• First of all, how does Paul describe the Scriptures?

• What significance do the Scriptures play in salvation according to this verse?

• Why do you think Paul used the word "wise" when talking about the Scriptures' impact?

• Through what does salvation come?

How does Luke describe those who obey the Word of God (Luke 11:28)?

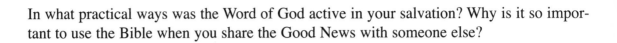
In what practical ways was the Word of God active in your salvation? Why is it so important to use the Bible when you share the Good News with someone else?

How would you describe regeneration? Who does the "work" of regeneration?

What are the essential themes of the Gospel given by the Apostle Paul? Why is the message of the Gospel considered "Good News"?

List several reasons why Christians should love the Bible. Whose portrait is painted in incredible detail in the Word of God?

If someone were to approach you with a question about salvation, how would you respond? What preparations have you made to share your faith with a lost person?

Have you developed a concise, personal testimony of your own conversion experience? Take some time to share your testimony with another believer. Ask for their feedback and advice on how to shorten it or make it better.

Make a list of the Bible verses that should be a part of everyone's evangelism tool belt. (The book of Romans is a great place to start.)

SESSION FOUR

THE WORD OF GOD PROVIDES LIFE-DIRECTION
4

Memory Verse: Psalm 119:105

Suppose I were to invite you on an expedition that would include a trip to the roof of the world—Mount Everest. The only immediate stipulation was that there would be no experienced guide for the journey, and the only way we would possibly be able to summit is to trust our natural mountain climbing abilities and our innate sense of direction. Do you think that you would want to join me on such a trip? Probably not. Why? Because climbing a mountain as dangerous as Everest requires experience, stamina, and someone who has been to the top before. You would be crazy, or at least misinformed, to join me on an expedition in which neither of us really knows how to get to the top. It would undoubtedly be a month long trek of motion without meaning.

The same is true for the Christian who decides to make the journey of life without so much as a peek into the Bible to find direction. You have been given the Word of God so that you can know for sure where you are headed and what you are supposed to be doing in preparation to summit this life. You do not have to rely on your own instincts or abilities to guide you. You have a surer Guide in the Holy Spirit, along with an inspired guidebook for life—the Bible. The Word of God provides a certain plan for life direction.

Have you ever searched the Scriptures to find God's direction for your life? Was your search successful? Why or why not?

What specific things did David ask God for in his prayer found in Psalm 25:4-5?

The specifics of God's will (direction) for your life may be a little bit harder to find in the Bible when you have not first surrendered to God's immediate will for your life. The Word of God is an open book to God's will for every person.

- God wants you to be saved. (Read 2 Peter 3:9.)
- God wants you to be filled with His Spirit. (Read Ephesians 5:15-18.)
- God wants you to be sanctified. (Read 1 Thessalonians 4:3, 4.)
- God want you to be submissive to His direction. (Read 1 Peter 2:13-15.)
- God wants you to be serving others. (Matthew 20:25-28.)
- God wants you to be willing to suffer for His sake. (Read 1 Peter 4:12-19.)

Are you saved, filled with His Spirit, sanctified, submissive, serving others, and willing to suffer? Because if you are, you can be confident that whatever you choose to do will be within God's plan for your life. That's right! If you are obedient to the Bible in these five areas, then God is already in control of your instincts and direction (Psalm 37:4). If you are a student of Scripture and a follower of Christ, then God's will does not have to be a mystery (Philippians 2:13).

But always be mindful of your fallen nature and its ability to regain its stronghold in your life. Remember, you may be obedient in all six of these areas, but before you begin to "climb Mount Everest," make sure your decision is bathed in prayer, guided by the Holy Spirit, discussed with mature spiritual counselors, and fully surrendered to God's purposes for your life. Remember, the climb may not be as important as your preparations for it. Allow the Word of God to provide you with wisdom and guidance in pursuing life direction.

According to Proverbs 16:9, what role does God play in leading and guiding our lives?

According to 1 John 5:14-15, what kind of prayer does God listen and respond to?

George Muller, a 19th century Christian and incredible man of faith from Bristol, England, used the following method when trying to determine life-direction. Notice his clear understanding of the importance of the Word of God:

1. I seek to get my heart into such a state that it has no will of its own in a given matter. When we are ready to do the Lord's will—whatever it may be—nine-tenths of the difficulties are overcome.

2. Having done this, I do not leave the result to simple feeling or simple impression. If I do so, I make myself liable to great delusions.

3. I seek the will of the Spirit of God through, or in connection with, God's Word. The Spirit and the Word must be combined. If I look to the Spirit alone without the Word, I lay myself open to great delusions also. If the Holy Spirit guides us, He will do it according to the Scriptures, never contrary to them.

4. Next I take into account providential circumstances. These often plainly indicate God's will in connection with His Word and Spirit.

5. I ask God in prayer to reveal His will to me.

6. Thus, through prayer, the study of the Word, and reflection, I come to a deliberate judgment according to the best of my ability and knowledge. If my mind is thus at peace and continues so after two or three more petitions, I proceed accordingly.

What principles emerge from the following verses that establish specific boundaries for knowing and doing God's will?

• **1 Corinthians 6:12:**

• **1 Corinthians 6:18:**

- **1 Corinthians 6:20:**

- **1 Corinthians 8:9:**

- **1 Corinthians 10:31:**

What lesson for discovering God's will for your life is found in Proverbs 3:5-6?

What role does the Holy Spirit have in helping you find life-direction (John 16:13)?

DISCUSSION QUESTIONS

SESSION FOUR

What verses in Scripture have been particularly encouraging to you when you were searching for God's will in a specific area of your life? Did these verses challenge your assumptions about God's will or change your direction altogether?

Do you really believe that God has a specific plan and purpose for every person? Why or why not?

Of the six things listed as God's will for every person, in what area do you struggle the most? Why?

Do you think George Muller's approach to determining life-direction is relevant to your life? What significance did the Word of God have in Muller's formula?

If there were one thing in your life that would keep you from doing the will of God, what would it be? What area of your life isn't fully surrendered to the purposes of God?

Do you think that finding God's will is possible? What has been your "system" for finding God's direction in the past?

Suppose you were offered a better job with better pay and bigger benefits, but taking the job meant relocating your family and leaving your place of service and ministry, what steps would you take in making that decision?

How has your concept of knowing God's will changed as a result of studying this lesson? How has it been strengthened?

THE WORD OF GOD PRODUCES SPIRITUAL GROWTH 5

Memory Verse: Psalm 119:89

Much of life is measured in terms of productivity. In fact, rarely, if ever, will you find a job in which certain demands of productivity are not part of the overall job description. Our culture measures people according to how productive they are—according to what they contribute. The reason for these external "measurements" is to ensure that what you are supposed to be doing is really being done. At work, the level of your compensation is due in large part to what you contribute to the organization.

As a Christian, when you come to the Word of God, you are called to a new level of spiritual productivity, because of the gracious contribution that has already been made on your behalf by Jesus Christ. Your "adoption" into the family of God carries with it, as part of the "job description," an assortment of opportunities that cannot be overlooked or carelessly disregarded. But the wonderful thing about your assignment is that it is recorded in detail in the Bible. And you have confidence that it can be accomplished because of those who have gone before you who have been quite successful in "bearing fruit."

What is the central point that James is making in James 1:22? What is the result of not only hearing the Word, but also doing what it says according to James 1:25?

Make a list of "fruit bearing" opportunities that you know are essential to your spiritual growth.

According to 2 Timothy 3:16, what are the four things, in order, that the Word of God provides you with?

1. _____ (What to believe and do)

2. _____ (Recognizing sin and disobedience)

3. _____ (How to change your life)

4. _____ (How to live your life)

What is the result of the application of Scripture on your life as stated in 2 Timothy 3:17?

What did Jesus reveal as the main problem with the religious leaders of His day (Matthew 22:29)?

What do the following verses teach about the importance of Scripture in the life of a growing Christian?

• **Psalm 1:2-3:**

• **Psalm 119:9-24:**

• **Hebrews 4:12:**

In His grace, Jesus never places demands on you that you are unable to meet. The living Word has given you the written Word and the Holy Spirit to enable you to grow deeper in the spiritual life. Jesus referred to Himself as the "vine" in John 15:1-8. This analogy that Jesus presented to His disciples was a powerful representation of their responsibility to bear fruit. But it also provided the small band of followers—the branches—with a sense of unity with the Vine—Jesus Christ. They knew that they were not called to bear fruit apart from the Vine. In fact, if they were to bear spiritual fruit of any kind, it would be a direct result of their union with the Vine and the pruning knife of the Word of God.

Read John 15:1-8 several times. Each time you read it, take notes that help you understand the message of this passage. And answer the following questions:

• **What role does Jesus play in this passage (verse 1)? What about God the Father (verse 1)?**

• **What does the Father do with branches that do not bear fruit on the vine (verse 2)?**

• **How are you "clean" according to verse 3?**

• **Whom do the branches represent (verse 5)?**

• **How do you bear fruit according to verse 5?**

• Who is glorified when you bear fruit (verse 8)?

The Word of God also provides you with a balanced diet of "spiritual food." This "spiritual food" is what provides the catalyst for your own spiritual growth. Take a moment to look up each passage and uncover the corresponding "food" that the Word provides.

• 1 Peter 2:2:

• Psalm 119:103:

• Hebrews 5:12-14:

• I Corinthians 3:1-2:

How important was the Word of God in Job's life according to Job 23:12?

What was Jeremiah's response to the Word of God in Jeremiah 15:16? What emotion did It produce?

What was the request of the Psalmist in the following verses?

• Psalm 119:34:

• Psalm 119:125:

• Psalm 119:169:

 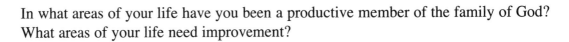

In what areas of your life have you been a productive member of the family of God? What areas of your life need improvement?

What are some specific ways in which you could alter your priorities and take advantage of opportunities that are available to you as a son or daughter of God?

Take a brief moment to write down where you spent most of your time last week. Based on the results, what amount of time do you currently spend doing God's work (i.e. ministry to the poor, Bible study, teaching, discipling, etc....)?

Why is bearing spiritual fruit impossible unless you are connected with the Vine—Jesus Christ?

What are some of the long-term goals of your spiritual life? Establish some accountability for these things and share your goals with another disciple.

What amount of time do you give to reading and studying the Word of God? How much more time could you invest in this discipline? What difference do you think this would make?

How has this study helped you understand the importance of the Word of God in producing spiritual growth?

SESSION SIX

GETTING THE MOST FROM GOD'S WORD

6

Memory Verse: James 1:22

Charles Spurgeon, the prince of preachers, said, "It is the Word that prunes the Christian. It is the truth that purges Him." Spiritual growth cannot take place apart from the Word of God. The message of the Bible is the life-giving force for the Christian. It sets spiritual expectations and provides a strategy for accomplishing God's purpose for your life. If you are in the Word of God with regularity, it will prune away those things in your life that separate you from a more intimate relationship with God. There certainly are clear benefits of reading and studying the Bible. Below are just a few:

- Studying the Bible gives substance to your faith.
- Studying the Bible equips you for life's trials.
- Studying the Bible allows you to handle it accurately.
- Studying the Bible enables you to distinguish truth from error.
- Studying the Bible inspires confidence in your walk with God.
- Studying the Bible reveals your purpose for living.

TAKING IT ALL IN

As part of your spiritual growth program, you should also make the following six disciplines a part of your regular intake of the Word of God:

1. **Hear the Word of God** (Proverbs 28:9; Luke 19:47-48). God's people have always been a hearing people, listening attentively to God's Word being proclaimed, taught, and preached.

2. **Read the Word of God** (Psalm 119:16; Revelation 1:3). Learn to enjoy reading the Word of God, absorbing its content, appreciating its relevance to living. Make it a daily habit to read God's Word and apply it to your life.

3. **Study the Word of God** (Proverbs 2:1-5; Acts 17:11). Studying the Bible goes beyond just reading the Word. When you study the Word of God, you are investigating further, digging deeper, writing down key principles and applications for living. If you are seeking to understand God's Word, intensive study will benefit you greatly.

4. **Memorize the Word of God** (Deuteronomy 6:6-7; Psalm 37:30-31; Psalm 119:9-11; Proverbs 7:1-3). Because it is beyond our human capacity to remember everything that we hear, read, and study, it is vital that we memorize. Memorizing portions of God's Word allows us to recall key passages and verses that can help both us and others during difficult times.

5. **Meditate on the Word of God** (Psalm 1:2-3; 119:15, 23, 48, 78, 97, 148). Meditation is a time to reflect on biblical truth or God's self-revelation in His Word. Meditation is as vital to reading the Word as exhaling is to breathing. Effective meditation is done prayerfully, listening for the inner teaching and promptings of the Holy Spirit.

6. **Obey the Word of God** (Psalm 119:55-56; Philippians 4:9; James 1:22-25). Effective use of the disciplines regarding God's Word cannot be accomplished without action. You will take action on what you really believe. God's Word should inspire us to obedience and action.

WHERE TO BEGIN

Begin today by setting aside a specific time to read and study the Word of God. Start by reading at least one chapter from John's Gospel per sitting. Once you have completed John, read Acts and Romans. Meditate on the words of the Psalmist in Psalm 119, the most celebrated passage in the Bible regarding the greatness of God's Word. From there return to the other Gospels—Matthew, Mark, and Luke—and become familiar with the life and ministry of Jesus Christ.

As you read, ask yourself these questions:

- What are the most important truths in this chapter?
- What do I learn about God, Jesus, or the Holy Spirit and my relationship to them?
- Is there an application for my life that I need to follow? A sin to avoid? Or a promise to claim?

Never fail to make prayer a vital part of your devotional life. In fact, prayer should be the beginning point and the ending point of every time spent studying the Word. Ask God to illuminate the pages of Scripture—to turn the spiritual light on (Psalm 119:18). Confess openly and honestly your sin. Present your needs as well as the needs of others. And praise Him for His goodness and greatness.

Also, you should become familiar with the following biblical accounts and their corresponding location in the Bible. These great passages will begin to ground you in the essential stories, truths, and promises of the Christian faith:

BIBLICAL ACCOUNT	LOCATION IN THE BIBLE
The Ten Commandments	Exodus 20
The Love Chapter	1 Corinthians 13
The Beatitudes	Matthew 5:1-12
The Parable of the Good Samaritan	Luke 10
The Two Great Commandments	Matthew 22:34-40
The Sermon on the Mount	Matthew 5-7
The Call of Abraham	Genesis 12
The Fall of Man	Genesis 3
The Golden Rule	Luke 6:31
The Parable of the Prodigal Son	Luke 15

Make the Bible the book you love—the book you can't live without. It should be a source of enduring joy and great inspiration. The Word of God will be the one place where you can go throughout your lifetime and continue to be challenged with life-changing truth and powerful application. Always remember, you hold in your hands the very Word of God—the inspired Manual of truth. Read it often. Trust it always. And live its message.

DAILY IN THE WORD

Daily in the Word is a very practical spiritual growth discipline that will assist you in deepening your relationship with God through His Word. It consists of five very simple steps. *See Appendix B for an example of a Daily In The Word journal entry.* Each of the following steps may be completed daily:

Step #1: Write the day and date on the page of a notebook or notepad.

Step #2: Write out a verse or series of verses that spoke to you during your Bible reading.

Step #3: Answer one or more of the following questions in your notebook:

- What sin should I avoid?
- What promise can I lean on?
- What command should I obey?
- What blessing can I enjoy?
- What lesson can I learn from?
- What victory has been promised?
- What aspect of God, Jesus, or the Holy Spirit was revealed?
- What attitude should I change?
- What path should I follow?
- What person should I speak to?

Step #4: Write out a prayer of commitment that reveals your response to the things the Lord has taught you.

- What does God want me to do?
- How should this passage change the way I think or live?
- How does this passage change my attitude?

Step #5: Exchange your spiritual journal with another Christ follower.

DISCUSSION QUESTIONS ?

SESSION SIX

Which one or two of the six benefits of studying the Bible is most relevant to your life right now? Why?

According to Joshua 1:8, what was Joshua's approach to meditating on the Word of God? What were the two benefits of this approach given at the end of this verse?

In which of the six disciplines for the regular intake of God's Word are you strongest? The weakest? What is your plan for improvement?

What were the Christians at Berea recognized for according to Acts 17:11? Why is this so important?

Read Psalm 1 together. What are the benefits of meditation taught in Psalm 1:3?

Why is it vital that we obey and do what the Word of God says? What is one of the benefits of being a "doer" of the Word (James 1:25)?

Who will teach and counsel us as we meditate on the Word of God? Does meditation involve silence or discussion, listening or talking?

How has your view of the Bible changed as a result of exploring God's Word in this section? How have you been changed?

[1] Charles R. Swindoll, *Growing Deep In The Christian Life* (Portland, Oregon: Multnomah Press, 1986), p. 62.

[2] R.C. Sproul, *Essential Truths Of The Christian Faith* (Wheaton, Illinois: Tyndale House Publishers, Inc., 1992), p. 16.

[3] Ibid., p. 171.

[4] Ibid., p. 172.

THE GODHEAD: KNOWING THE ONE WHO MATTERS MOST

INTRODUCTION

As a disciple of Jesus Christ, there is nothing more important to your Christian life than what you think and know about God. Remember, He is the center of all that exists. He is life. He is the Creator and Sustainer of all that is and all that will be. Much of what you will learn about Him is beyond human comprehension, but it is an expression of your faith that allows you to understand and know and become focused on the living God.

Unless God becomes the primary pursuit of your life, all other pursuits will not satisfy. They will not work. They will not bring fulfillment. And you will never fully know yourself, who God made you to be, until you begin the exciting adventure of knowing Him. I can personally guarantee you that it will be worth your time to explore the truths of His Word and see His nature revealed.

Consider yourself fortunate, because God has chosen to reveal Himself through creation, the Bible, His Son Jesus Christ, and through the Holy Spirit. He has given you a mountain of revelation from which to draw a deeper and fuller understanding of who He is—so what are you waiting for? Dig in and uncover the treasure of knowing God. But before you begin, allow me to share five important reasons for knowing Him.

1. Knowing God exposes the truth about who you are (Isaiah 6:1-5).
2. Knowing God enables you to have an eternal perspective (I Corinthians 2:9).
3. Knowing God gives you the passion to be like Him (Jeremiah 9:24).
4. Knowing God allows you to understand your world (Daniel 4:35).
5. Knowing God gives you strength and confidence (Daniel 11:32).

SESSION ONE

GOD THE FATHER

Memory Verse: Romans 8:28

WHO IS GOD?

While 90% of Americans may believe, according to Gallup and other polls, that there is a god or "Higher Power," less and less people are making faith an important part of their lives. So the proof of the polling reveals that this "Higher Power" has no impact on people's day-to-day existence. You can be certain that the "Higher Power" being spoken of in the polls is not the God of the Bible, because from Genesis to Revelation He is constantly changing and rearranging people's lives to accommodate His redemptive purposes. God is always at work in your life, molding and shaping you into the image of His Son—Jesus Christ (Romans 8:29).

Based on what you may have already learned or know about God, how would you describe Him to someone who had never heard of Him before? Include as many characteristics and names of God as you know.

GOD IS REVEALED IN HIS WORD

By now you are probably familiar with Paul's word to Timothy in 2 Timothy 3:16-17 regarding the inspiration of Scripture and its subsequent benefit to your life. The inspired Bible is God's complete revelation of Himself to you and to the rest of humanity. God can be seen and known throughout the pages of His Word. When you fully acknowledge the Bible as God's love letter to you, you will find its pages irresistible, its truths remarkable, and its life-changing force completely persuasive. Furthermore, when you have a fresh encounter with God through His Word, He is revealing more about Himself to you in a very real and relevant way.

What verse or passage in Scripture has God used to reveal Himself to you recently? Did you acknowledge God's self-revelation in that encounter?

Read Ephesians 6:17. According to this verse, what is the sword of the Spirit?

FINDING GOD IN THE PROVERBS

The Book of Proverbs reveals many of the characteristics of God. Knowing who He is and what He does will allow you to be confident in His provision and His calling on your life.

CHARACTERISTIC OF GOD	LOCATION IN PROVERBS
God is aware of everything	Proverbs 15:3
God knows people's hearts	Proverbs 15:11; 21:2
God controls everything	Proverbs 16:33; 21:30
God is a place of safety	Proverbs 18:10
God rescues the righteous	Proverbs 11:8, 21
God condemns the wicked	Proverbs 11:31
God listens to our prayers	Proverbs 15:8, 29
God loves those who pursue righteousness	Proverbs 15:9
God cares for the poor and needy	Proverbs 22:22-23
God tests our hearts	Proverbs 17:3

Of the many characteristics of God that you find in Proverbs, which one or two mean the most to you? Why?

FINDING GOD IN THE PSALMS

The Book of Psalms is rich with references about God. Again we find the Word of God revealing the truth about who God is. The following list of word pictures gives you an unrestricted view into the multi-faceted nature of God:

WORD PICTURE USED FOR GOD	LOCATION IN PSALMS
Rock	Psalm 18:2, 31
Fortress	Psalm 31:3; 91:2
Deliverer	Psalm 40:17; 70:5
Shield	Psalm 144:2
Refuge	Psalm 9:9; 14:6
Shepherd	Psalm 23:1; 80:1
Light	Psalm 44:3; 90:8
Salvation	Psalm 51:12; 62:2

What word pictures about God are the most relevant in your life right now? Why?

Read Psalm 139. List at least three characteristics of God that are revealed to you in this psalm.

1.

2.

3.

DISCUSSION QUESTIONS ?

SESSION ONE

List some of the everyday distractions that keep believers from knowing God. Were any of these distractions present when you first began "pursuing" a relationship with your spouse or best friend? How did you avoid these distractions?

Of the five reasons for knowing God given in the introduction, which one really forced you to evaluate your current relationship with Him? Why?

How would you describe the apparent gap between people believing in a "Higher Power" and the inability of that "Higher Power" to redirect, change, and impact their lives? How does the God of the Bible differ from a perceived "Higher Power"?

How much of what you currently believe about God has been a result of daily encounters with Him through His Word and prayer? How much of what you believe has come as a result of someone else's experience, teaching, or preaching?

What practical steps can you take to invest more time and energy in your relationship with God? What things might have to be avoided or forgotten in order to know God?

What does Psalm 86:5 and Psalm 116:5 reveal about the nature of God? Write down as many attributes of God as you can from these verses.

In your life, how has God shown Himself to be consistent with His character as revealed in Scripture?

FINDING GOD IN THE REST OF THE BIBLE

Memory Verse: Isaiah 40:31

In His goodness, God has revealed Himself in other parts of Scripture as well. In the following passages He is known as:

- The mighty God (Isaiah 9:6)
- Our Father (Isaiah 64:8)
- The God of all comfort (2 Corinthians 1:3)
- The Head of the Church (Ephesians 5:23)
- Lord of the Harvest (Matthew 9:38)

- Faithful and True (Revelation 19:11)
- A sure Foundation (Isaiah 28:16)
- Our Captain (2 Chronicles 13:12)
- Righteous Judge (2 Timothy 4:8)
- The Potter (Isaiah 64:8)

The Bible is rich with the revelation of who God is. When God spoke in Scripture, it was intended to reveal something about Himself, His purposes, or His ways. His whole intention in revealing Himself to you is to bring you into a lifelong relationship with Him. You may never fully understand His methods or particular actions, but you can be confident that when God is being gracious enough to show you who He is in Scripture, He is trying to draw you into a deeper and more meaningful relationship with Him.

Read Isaiah 55:8. What is God revealing about Himself in this particular verse? How does this verse reveal the truth about man's ways? (Read Proverbs 16:2.)

As you read Micah 4:2, what does this verse tell you that God will teach you? How would you describe this teaching process?

What does Malachi 3:6 reveal to you about the nature of God?

In Leviticus19:1-2, what is another characteristic of God that He revealed in Scripture?

A BIBLICAL PERSPECTIVE OF GOD

1. **GOD IS SELF-EXISTENT.** You may have noticed that the Bible makes no attempt to prove God's existence. The Bible teaches that a knowledge of God is woven into the very fabric of human consciousness. This might explain the endless search for meaning and purpose that so many people are pursuing. A quest of this nature only occurs because deep in our hearts we are incurably persuaded that God does exist—that He is there (Romans 1:19-20; Psalm 19:1-4). But because of sin no one seeks after God on His own initiative (Romans 3:10-12). God must tenderly draw people to Himself.

As you read Genesis 1:1, do you find the writer attempting to prove God's existence?

According to Hebrews 3:4, who built everything that exists?

2. **GOD EXISTS IN THREE PERSONS.** There is only one God. He is one in essence but plural in distinctions of His personality. The Old Testament affirms this truth in the use of the Hebrew word *Elohim*. This is a name for God that we find used about 2,600 times in the Old Testament, and it is plural in form. God even referred to Himself in the plural form in the Bible (Genesis 1:26; 3:22).

To fully know God, you must acknowledge His triune nature—that He is Three in One. This is a difficult concept to grasp, but it is essential to understanding God. We serve sons—God the Father, God the Son (Jesus), and God the Holy Spirit. Whenever God is working, all three members of the Godhead are working.

The New Testament also affirms that there is one God, and yet shows God existing as Father, Son, and Holy Spirit:

- God the Father (2 Peter 1:17; 1 Thessalonians 1:1)

- God the Son (I John 5:20; Titus 2:13; John 1:1, 14)

- God the Holy Spirit (2 Corinthians 3:17; Acts 5:3-4)

> *Webster defines the "Trinity" as "the unity of the Father, Son, and Holy Spirit as three persons in one godhead."*

3. **GOD IS A SPIRIT.** God is an invisible Spirit Who is not bound by the same constraints as we are—space, time, and form. Throughout the Bible He revealed Himself to people in multiple forms—as a man, through a voice, in thunder or lightning, even in a burning bush. He can manifest Himself in any way He sees fit. Remember, He is all-powerful and has power over His entire creation, which means that He can reveal Himself in whatever form would best serve His purposes.

Read John 4:24. What does this verse tell you about God?

According to Isaiah 46:9, do any gods exist besides God?

What are the two names used to describe God in Isaiah 57:15?

1.

2.

How long has God existed according to Isaiah 57:15?

SESSION TWO

What is God's whole intention for revealing Himself in Scripture? Why does He do this, according to John 15:16?

How do Jeremiah 31:3 and Hosea 11:4 describe the way in which God draws us to Himself?

If you were to stand before God, would you be able to say that you love Him with all of your heart, soul, mind, and strength (Deuteronomy 6:4-5; Mark 12:30)? What would prevent you from saying that?

What do you think it means to love God with all of your heart, soul, mind, and strength? How would you describe the depths of this love? In what practical ways can you live out this kind of love?

How would you describe the triune nature of God? Who are the three Members of the Godhead?

What Hebrew word is used throughout the Old Testament that affirms the plurality of God? What verse in Genesis 1 reveals that the triune God was present at creation?

Why is it so important for us to understand that God is a spirit? How should this affect our worship of God (Philippians 3:3)?

What is one thing that you learned about God while completing this study?

THE ATTRIBUTES OF GOD

Memory Verse: 1 John 4:7-8

GOD IS LOVE

So who is God? God is who He says He is. The Bible reveals hundreds of names for God, each of which reveal a certain attribute that tells you something specific about His nature. And God is also who others in the Bible say He is. This is one of the reasons why we see new names or titles for God after an event where a Bible character had an encounter with Him. But perhaps the most important definition of who God is can be found in I John 4:7-8. In this passage, the Word of God tells us that "God is love." This is who God is. He is love. His very nature is love, and He will never express His will or plan to you without being true and faithful to the love He has for you. He wants what is best for you. Therefore, God will never give you second best—never!

At this point, how would you define love? Do you think your definition of love is biblically accurate?

Read I Corinthians 13, the "love" chapter, and write down every characteristic of real love that you can find. As you compile your list, keep in mind that this is just the beginning of God's love for you.

How would you currently describe your understanding of the love of God? (Check a box.)

❏ I'm not really sure

❏ I'm a little bit confused about His love and His wrath

❏ I feel like I don't deserve His love

❏ I know that I need to share His love with others

❏ I am confident that God's love always wants what is best for me

Never underestimate the importance of trusting in the loving nature of God. You will face many circumstances in life where it will be difficult, perhaps close to impossible, to see God's love being manifested, but you must be confident that through every situation, He loves you. He wants what is best for you, and His love demands that He give you only what is best. God would be less than who He says He is, if He ceased to express Himself in any other way besides perfect love. And the greatest expression of His perfect love was revealed at the cross (John 3:16; 1 John 3:16).

Before you go any further, is there any question in your heart or mind about the depths of God's love for you? (Check a box.)

❏ No, I fully believe that God loves me, and He wants what is best.

❏ Yes, I am still not able to totally accept His loving nature.

Write out Romans 8:28 below. What reassurance do you get from this verse?

GOD IS ALL-KNOWING

Theologians will often use the word *omniscient* to describe the fact that God is all-knowing. God is the possessor of all knowledge—whether past, present, or future. You will have a much easier time of trusting in God and believing what He says when you confidently believe in the omniscience of God. Ultimately, this truth will be a great source of security when you find yourself pursuing a particular life-direction. However, God's all-knowing character also highlights the fact that we cannot hide from God. Everything is exposed in the light of God's omniscience (Hebrews 4:13), and no corner of the world escapes His watchful eye. He is God, and He is all-knowing.

What does Psalm 147:5 reveal to you about God's understanding? How does this compare to the understanding of man?

Read Ezekiel 11:5. How does this verse reveal the omniscience of God? What implications does this verse have on how you think (your thought life)?

The all-knowing nature of God is also significant when you consider His ability to judge righteously and fairly (Nehemiah 9:32-33; 2 Timothy 4:1, 8). For the Judge to deliver a reasonable and fair verdict, He must be fully aware of all the evidence. You can be sure that there is no piece of evidence hidden from God's eyes. He knows everything.

Because God is infinite (without limit or end) in His knowledge, three important thoughts should always be remembered:

1. God is aware of everything.
2. God understands everything.
3. God comprehends everything.

GOD IS ALL-POWERFUL

When you consider the all-powerful nature of God, you should remember the word *omnipotence*. This word refers to God holding all power over His whole creation. Nothing stands outside the reach of His full control. What may be impossible for you is possible with Him. He is sovereign over all, and there is nothing that can confine His power (Romans 11:36). As a Christ-follower, you have at your disposal the same power that God displayed in creation. And because of that incredible power, there is nothing that can thwart His plans and purposes for your life (Luke 1:37).

What does Job 42:2 teach you about God's omnipotence?

In Psalm 115:3, what does the psalmist tell you about God's authority over creation?

According to Ephesians 1:11, how does God work everything out?

God's all-powerful nature empowers you to accomplish His purposes. When you have been led to accomplish something that is beyond your power or that exceeds your resources, you can be almost sure that it is God leading you to do it. If He purposes to do something, He will do it (Isaiah 46:10-11). You just need to believe in simple, childlike faith that the God who is powerful over all of His creation is able to empower you to do everything that He asks of you. He loves to use ordinary people to accomplish His plan. That has always been His pattern in Scripture. Consider the following examples:

- God empowered Noah and his sons to build an ark for the purpose of sparing the lives of Noah's family, as well as every animal species (Genesis 6-9).
- God empowered Gideon and 300 ordinary men to defeat an army of 120,000 (Judges 7-8).
- God empowered Paul to carry the gospel all the way to Rome (Acts 28:16).

God is also holy (Psalm 99), just (Genesis 18:25), good (James 1:17), and fully present in every place—omnipresent (Jeremiah 23:23-24). You will never exhaust the endless quest to know who God is, but you can begin, day by day, to develop an intimate relationship with Him. This is the only way that you can begin to know Him. This study will provide you with a more thorough knowledge of God, but it will never serve as a replacement for a life fully devoted to knowing Him, to trusting Him, and to serving His purposes.

According to Acts 17:24-25, what is God's connection to everything that exists?

SESSION THREE

Why do you think it is so important to understand the loving nature of God? In what practical ways has He chosen to reveal His loving nature?

According to 1 John 3:16, how do we understand the depths of God's love? How do we express our love for Him (John 14:21; 1 John 3:16, 18)?

Define the word *omniscient*. What does Romans 11:33-36 teach about the omniscience of God?

Why is God's omniscience a critical factor in His role as Judge? How does 2 Timothy 4:8 describe Him as a Judge?

Why does God's omniscience challenge us to live more holy lives?

What does the word *omnipotence* mean? How is God's omnipotence a source of comfort for those who love Him (Luke 1:37)?

Which attribute of God means the most to you? Why? What is an additional characteristic of the nature of God revealed in Deuteronomy 6:15?

SESSION FOUR

GOD THE SON

4

Memory Verse: 1 Timothy 3:16

WHO IS JESUS?

Whether skeptic or saint, most people would agree that Jesus, a carpenter's son from Nazareth, was the most influential person that ever lived. His transformational teachings and exemplary life have transcended time and culture. And His story, as unbelievable as it may be, has been told and retold by more people than any other in recorded history. Still more amazing is the fact that He impacted the world with a force unmatched by any other in only thirty-three short years of life. And it was only the last three years of His life that were given to any sort of "public" ministry. How then could this virgin-born son of a carpenter turn the world upside down without money, armies, or the cultural elite at His disposal? How could someone born in a manger and crucified as a criminal control the destiny of the civilized world and rule a spiritual kingdom that embraces one-third of the world's population?

What does 1 Timothy 3:16 say about how God revealed Himself?

Whom did God reveal Himself through (John 1:14, 17)? And Whom did Jesus come from (John 1:14)?

According to Galatians 4:4, who is Jesus?

All of the questions you may have about who Jesus is can be answered through the Word of God. Jesus is the Son of God, while at the same time Jesus is God. God took on human form and lived among us through the person of His Son Jesus Christ. (The term *Christ* literally means "Messiah.") In this unique self-revelation, God's deity and our humanity were perfectly combined to create the God-man—Jesus Christ (1 Timothy 2:5). It begins to defy our finite comprehension to think that God Himself took on our humanity to become like us in all things except sin (Hebrews 4:15), and yet Jesus Himself referred to Himself as the Son of Man scores of times throughout the Gospels (Matthew 16:13).

Do you understand the impact of God's self-revelation through His Son Jesus Christ?

❑ **Yes, I am thoroughly convinced that Jesus was God in the flesh.**

❑ **No, I do not fully understand how or why God became a man.**

WAS JESUS HUMAN?

Though Jesus was fully and eternally God, He was also the *"man Christ Jesus"* (1 Timothy 2:5). For God to take on human flesh was necessary for several reasons—not the least of which was to accomplish His purposes to redeem lost and sinful man.

According to Hebrews 2:17-18, why was it necessary for Jesus to become a human being?

What does Hebrews 2:18 tell you about Jesus' humanity?

As you read Hebrews 2:14, what further task was Jesus accomplishing through His death on the cross?

Jesus' death on the cross was significant, not only because it made atonement for our sins, but also because it destroyed forever the power of death and Satan. Christ's humanity gave Him the opportunity to experience the very real forces that were at work in this world through the influence and power of Satan (the serpent found in Genesis 3).

Read Hebrews 4:14-15. These verses tell us how Jesus was both like us and different.

How was Jesus like us?

How was Jesus different?

Why do you think it was important for Jesus to share similar experiences with us, yet remain untouched by sin?

According to the following verses, what are the human feelings that Jesus shared with us?

REFERENCE	FEELING JESUS SHARED
Matthew 21:18	
John 4:6	
John 19:28	
Hebrews 4:15	
John 11:35	

When you consider the humanity of Jesus, it is also important to remember that He had human parents and a lineage that traced back through King David to Adam (Luke 3:23-38). Jesus also had a normal human body (Romans 8:3; John 4:9) that grew just like yours (Luke 2:40, 52) but was never tainted by sin (Hebrews 4:15). Jesus' humanity also paints a picture for us of what our fellowship with God would have been like had we remained untouched by sin. Jesus experienced intimate communion with the Father, like no other human being before or since.

You have just learned about Jesus' humanity. Is there anything that remains unclear to you about God the Son becoming a man?

Read Philippians 2:5-11 and answer the following questions:

• **Who was Jesus according to verse 6?**

• **According to verse 7, what form or likeness did Jesus take on?**

• **What did Jesus look like according to verse 8?**

- After Jesus became a man, what two steps preceded His death on the cross (verse 8)?

1.

2.

- What was God's response to Jesus' death and resurrection (verse 9)?

- What two things will every human being do before Jesus according to verses 10-11?

1.

2.

- Who is glorified through the life, death, and resurrection of the Son of God (verse 11)?

SESSION FOUR

How is Jesus Christ described in Colossians 1:15? Whom does Jesus say that He is according to John 10:38?

Why was it necessary for God to take on human flesh? How are believers reconciled to God (Colossians 1:22)?

How does Isaiah's prophecy support the claim that the coming Messiah would be both fully human and fully God (Isaiah 9:6)?

Read Matthew 16:13-17 together. Who did Simon Peter say that Jesus was (verse 16)? Who revealed this truth to Him (verse 17)? Do you think it would be fair to say that the Holy Spirit is responsible for revealing this truth to us? Why or why not?

If Jesus had come to this world and sinned, would His death on the cross have been able to satisfy the sacrificial demands of God? Why not?

When God was revealed in the flesh, what two groups of people rejected Him (John 1:10-11)?

As His disciples, why can we confidently approach the throne (Hebrews 4:15)? How is this truth a comfort to us when we struggle and fail?

THE DEITY AND DESTINY OF JESUS

5

Memory Verse: John 1:14

WAS JESUS GOD?

The Word of God tells us that Jesus was God revealed in the flesh (1 Timothy 3:16). Colossians 1:15 makes known that Christ was the "image of the invisible God." It is hard to imagine that God came in the flesh (John 1:1, 14), and yet the world did not even know that it was Him (John 1:10). In fact, the Bible points out that His own people did not receive Him (John 1:11). He was rejected by those He came to save.

The references in Scripture that point to Jesus as God are many. Consider the following:

Jesus is called God	John 1:1, 14; 20:28; Romans 9:5
Jesus is called the Son of God	John 1:14, 18; 3:16
Jesus bears the divine names of God	Revelation 1:8, 17; 22:13; John 8:24, 58
Jesus is worshiped as God	Matthew 14:33; John 20:28; Hebrews 1:6
Jesus is to be equally honored as God	John 5:23; Isaiah 42:8

Jesus shares the divine offices
- Creator — Colossians 1:15-17; Hebrews 1:2, 10
- Judge — John 5:22
- Forgiver of sins — Matthew 9:2-6

Jesus has life in himself — John 5:26

Jesus shares the divine attributes
- He is unchangeable — Hebrews 13:8
- He is all-powerful (omnipotent) — Revelation 1:8
- He is all-knowing (omniscient) — John 21:17
- He is all-present (omnipresent) — Matthew 28:20
- He is eternal — 1 Timothy 1:16-17

Deity means "God" or "Supreme Being"

Jesus did the works of God
- He had authority over nature — Matthew 8:26-27; Mark 4:39-41
- He created food — Matthew 14:19-21; 15:36-38
- He raised the dead — John 11:32-44; Luke 7:12-16

In John 5:21, 40, Jesus claims the power to give what? What do you think He means?

Read John 10:28-33. What were Jesus' claims in verses 28 and 30? Why do you think He was met with such resistance in verses 31-33?

Do you think that the average person's response to the claims of Christ are any different two thousand years later? What was your first response to the truth of the Gospel?

WHOM DID JESUS CLAIM TO BE?

Jesus understood His role as Prophet (Mark 6:4; Acts 3:22), Priest (Hebrews 4:14-16; 7:24-25), and King (Revelation 19:16; John 19:19). He knew that He was the greatest prophet of all, and that He was the one that Moses spoke of in Deuteronomy 18:15-19. Yet He also understood the significance of being a representative of His people before God the Father in His role as Priest—a role spoken of in 1 Samuel 2:35. But perhaps His greatest role would be as King. In His spiritual kingdom there is no name greater, and in a coming time He will be acknowledged by all as Lord, Master, and King (Philippians 2:5-11). Although Jesus fills all three of these offices right now, He has also emphasized that He is much more than just our Great Prophet, Priest, and King. On the following page, investigate further the seven "I am" statements that Jesus made about Himself and their significance to your life.

Read the following verses and write the name Christ gave Himself next to each:

REFERENCE	NAME/CLAIM	SIGNIFICANCE FOR YOU
John 6:35	_____	Refers to Jesus' role as the only source of eternal life.
John 8:12	_____	Refers to Jesus' role as the answer for our need for spiritual truth.
John 10:7	_____	Refers to Jesus' role as the only way into God's kingdom.
John 10:11	_____	Refers to Jesus' role as the Messiah, providing love and direction.
John 11:25	_____	Refers to Jesus' role as the source of life and the power over death.
John 14:6	_____	Refers to Jesus' role as the Savior and Redeemer of mankind.
John 15:1	_____	Refers to Jesus' role as the source of all spritual growth and life.

Can you confidently affirm that Jesus Christ was God in human flesh?

❑ **Yes, I believe that Jesus is who He claims to be.**

❑ **No, I do not believe that Jesus is who He claims to be.**

WHY DID JESUS COME?

Jesus' purpose for coming to this sin-stained planet was so that humanity could be restored to a right relationship with God. This process of restoration, known as salvation, could only be done through Jesus' sacrifice on the cross. But His death alone was not enough to redeem us. His resurrection also plays a vital role in our justification (*justification* refers to you being made right with God—Colossians 2:14) (Romans 4:25).

What was Jesus' mission according to Luke 19:10? According to Matthew 1:21?

Why did the Father send His Son into the world (1 John 4:14)?

As you read the following verses, consider how fully Jesus completed the work which He was sent to do:

Romans 8:3-4	Jesus' sacrifice met the full demands of the law against us.
Acts 13:39	Jesus' sacrifice justified us from everything from which we could not be justified.
Romans 8:1	Jesus' sacrifice frees us from all past, present, and future condemnation.
John 12:32-33; 1 John 2:2	Jesus' sacrifice was enough to save all sinners. But they still must receive Him.
Hebrews 10:12	Jesus' sacrifice satisfied the demands of His Father once and for all.

Jesus Christ, the God-man from Nazareth, forever changed the way lost sinners find a Savior. In His life, He embodied all of the essence of deity, while remaining completely human. In His death on the cross, He bore the weight of all our sins, so that we might be made righteous before God.

Jesus' life was consumed with a singular purpose and passion to redeem a lost world, but He went beyond that. He also modeled for us a selfless lifestyle. He was willing to suffer and die to fulfill His Father's mission and leave for us an example of complete and total surrender. And in His resurrection, He was exalted to His rightful place at His Father's right hand, so that He could serve as our Mediator, our faithful High Priest, and our God.

Write a one or two sentence description of who Jesus is based on what you have just learned from His Word.

As you read John 1:1-18, what important facts emerge about "the Word" in these verses? List as many as you can.

Would the promise of John 10:28-29 mean anything if Jesus were simply a man and not God? Why not?

Which one of the seven "I am" statements that Jesus made is the most important to you? Why? Was there a time in your life when one of the "I am" statements was a particular comfort to you?

How is the "true bread from heaven" greater than the manna in the wilderness (John 6:32-35; 48-51; 54-58)? Contrast the differences between "true bread" and manna.

What does the word *justification* mean? How did Jesus justify us before God?

According to Mark 2:17, what purpose did Jesus give His disciples for His coming? Answering honestly, have you ever doubted the salvation of someone who was living a particularly sinful lifestyle? Understanding the mission of Jesus, do you still have doubts?

Write a one-sentence statement describing the purpose that Jesus had for coming to earth.

GOD THE HOLY SPIRIT

Memory Verse: Psalm 51:10-11

WHO IS THE HOLY SPIRIT?

The Holy Spirit is one of the members of the Triune God. While we worship one Lord, He is expressed as Father, Son, and Holy Spirit. The Holy Spirit has the names of God (Acts 5:3-4), the attributes of God (Psalm 139:7-10), and full honor as God (Matthew 12:31-32). The Holy Spirit was present at Creation (Genesis 1:2), and He was the One who inspired the written Word (2 Peter 1:21).

You cannot understand the truths of the Word of God unless the Holy Spirit reveals them to you. If you are unaided by the Holy Spirit, the ways and things of God are foolishness to you (1 Corinthians 2:14). Enabled by the Spirit, you can understand all things (1 Corinthians 2:15).

There are several images of the Holy Sprit that are used in Scripture. These images allow us to understand His person and work. Consider the following examples:

• What image is associated with the Holy Spirit in John 3:8 and Acts 2:2?

• What image is associated with the Holy Spirit in John 7:38-39?

• What image is associated with the Holy Spirit in John 1:32?

• What image is associated with the Holy Spirit in Acts 2:3-4?

• What image is associated with the Holy Spirit in 1 John 2:20, 27?

WHAT DOES THE HOLY SPIRIT DO?

The Holy Spirit's primary ministry is one of empowering believers and enabling them to understand truth and accomplish God's purposes in the world. Because of the importance of the work that the Spirit accomplishes, Jesus asked the Father to give believers the Spirit permanently (John 14:16). The first account of the permanent indwelling of the Holy Spirit in the lives of believers took place at Pentecost (Acts 2:1-4), just as Jesus had predicted (John 14:17).

This indwelling of the Holy Spirit was exclusive to the body of Christ that was forming after Christ's resurrection and ascension. Prior to Pentecost, no abiding presence was available to believers. The Spirit simply empowered people for certain tasks (i.e. Samson—Judges 13:24-25; craftsman of the Tabernacle—Exodus 35:30-35). That is one reason why King David asked God not to take His Holy Spirit from Him (Psalm 51:11).

This lasting indwelling of the Holy Spirit that is available to us now gives us a decided advantage in our walk with God, in our ministry within the church, and our impact outside of it. He is always with us, guiding us into all truth. The Holy Spirit will never abandon us, if we are truly God's children.

The Holy Sprit of God accomplishes several important tasks:

1. Everything is accomplished through the Holy Spirit's power—creation (Genesis 1:2; Psalm 104:30); Christ's resurrection (Romans 8:11); miracles (Matthew 12:28).
2. The Holy Spirit is the revealer of God to us—He is the Teacher, Illuminator, and Guide (John 16:13; Romans 8:14).
3. The Holy Spirit brings spiritual life to us—He convicts us of sin (John 16:8); and He regenerates (John 3:5) and enables us to see spiritual truth.
4. The Holy Spirit was the means of conception in the life of the Son of God (Luke 1:35).
5. The Holy Spirit blesses us with spiritual gifts (1 Corinthians 12).

What are some of the Holy Spirit's activities mentioned in the following verses?

REFERENCE	HOLY SPIRIT'S ACTIVITY
Genesis 1:2	
John 3:5-6	
John 16:7-11	
John 16:13-14	
2 Peter 1:21	

What are the fruits of the Spirit (marks of a spirit-filled life) that are listed in Galatians 5:22-23? Are these fruits present in your life?

What name is given to the Holy Spirit in John 14:26? What two things will the Holy Spirit do according to this verse?

According to Acts 1:8, what do you receive through the Holy Spirit?

According to the following verses, how does the Holy Spirit work in you after you are saved?

• Romans 8:14:

• Romans 8:26-27:

• John 16:13:

Make a list of the spiritual gifts that the Holy Spirit distributes to believers in 1 Corinthians 12. What gift or gifts do you think He has given you?

The presence of God the Holy Spirit means that the permanent indwelling of Christ is within us. Every believer has the mind of Christ, the guidance of Christ, and the power of Christ forever through the gift of the Holy Spirit. But even though we have all this within our grasp, we still need one another, so the Spirit unites us as one Body and gives us gifts which are intended to build each other up. We were not designed to journey through this life alone, but with one another, empowered forever by the Holy Spirit. Our best intentions and most well planned strategies will always fall short if the Holy Spirit is not the enabling agent in them. We need Him, and that is the very reason why Christ prayed to His Father to give Him to us.

DISCUSSION QUESTIONS

SESSION SIX

What is the promise that Jesus Christ made to every believer in John 16:7? Why did Jesus have such a high regard for the Holy Spirit?

How does the permanent indwelling of the Holy Spirit compare to the physical presence of Jesus that the disciples enjoyed? If you were one of His disciples at the time, how would you have reacted to Jesus' statement in John 16:16?

Why is the Holy Spirit such an important part of our own spiritual growth process? At what event in the Bible did the Holy Spirit begin to permanently indwell believers?

According to John 7:38-39, what event had to precede the coming of the Holy Spirit?

How can you measure the power of the Holy Spirit working in you according to Galatians 5:22-23? Of the fruits listed in these two verses, which ones are blossoming in your life? Which need more work?

What work does the Holy Spirit accomplish in us? Why would it be impossible to change without the Holy Spirit?

What function does the Holy Spirit perform when we are reading and studying the Word of God? Why is this so vital to our spiritual progress?

Describe the work of the Holy Spirit in a one or two sentence statement.

3

THE CHRISTIAN LIFE: CHOOSING THE PATH OF FULL DEVOTION

INTRODUCTION

The Christian life places you on the path with Jesus Christ, a path of Holy Spirit enabling and constant companionship with God through His Son. Being in the way (Acts 18:25-26) of Christ will involve self-denial and obedience (Luke 9:23). For some, it may mean forfeiture of plans and dreams, in favor of a life fully surrendered to the destiny that God has chosen. For others, it will mean a reprioritizing of goals and successes, and a Christ-centered reevaluation of what total discipleship means. For all of us though, the Christian life dictates a change of nature and character that can only be described as supernatural (2 Corinthians 5:17).

We have not initiated our relationship with God, but He has divinely intervened in our lives to draw us to Himself (John 6:44). Our only appropriate response when God steps into our lives in this way is to answer immediately with the "wherever, whatever" reply that we see so often throughout the pages of Scripture (Matthew 4:18-22). This answer is always given when you understand that God not only commands the body you dwell in, but also the life you live. His call is always one of redirection and reprioritization. It not only demands obedience, but also complete surrender. So wave your white flag towards the heavens and let God know you're His—completely, totally, without regret.

This is the Christian life, and this is the path that God has placed you on. The degree to which you succeed or fail at following Christ will hinge completely on your dependence on your Guide (John 15:5). You cannot succeed in the Christ-life, if your energies and passions are given to following your own self-directed choices and decisions. So make your mind up to follow Christ with total abandon, for in Him is life (John 3:36).

THE IMPACT OF THE NEW BIRTH

Memory Verse: 2 Corinthians 5:17

When Jesus Christ was approached by Nicodemus in John 3, He told Nicodemus that he would have to be *"born again"* (John 3:3) to see the kingdom of God. This statement surprised Nicodemus, because he did not understand that Jesus was talking about a spiritual rebirth, not a physical one (John 3:4-6). Nicodemus was unaware, despite his familiarity with Old Testament teachings, that being *"born again"* is a phrase applied to a person when he or she becomes a member of the family of God (John 3:10). (The source of this rebirth that Jesus spoke about is God and not man (John 1:13).)

The new birth that Jesus spoke of means that a person who is born again receives *a new nature* (a spiritual one; 2 Corinthians 5:17); *a new life* (eternal life; 1 John 5:11-12); *a new family* (the family of God; 1 John 3:1); *a new freedom* (freedom from sin; Romans 6:12-13); and *a new power* (the Spirit of God; Romans 8:9). But the new birth doesn't happen by itself. There are two forces at work that bring about a spiritual rebirth:

1. **The Word of God** (1 Peter 1:23; James 1:18). The Bible is the seed of our salvation (Matthew 13:18-23), and through belief and obedience to the Word of God, the new birth comes.

2. **The Spirit of God** (Titus 3:5). The Holy Spirit is the member of the Godhead who convicts us of our sin and leads us to Jesus Christ for salvation. Being born again could not happen apart from the Holy Spirit's divine intervention.

THE FAMILY TREE

There are only two spiritual families that exist. One is the family of Adam. The other is the family of God. Every person belongs to one of these two families. In the Bible, the sinful nature belonging to those in the family of Adam is known as the old man (or self), while the nature belonging to members of God's family is referred to as the new man (or self). Each phrase makes a distinction between our past (unsaved) and our present (saved) position before God. And our standing before God rests solely on the work of Jesus Christ (Hebrews 10:10, 14)

The old man is all that we inherited from Adam (Romans 5:12, 19), our original, fallen parent (Ephesians 4:22; Colossians 3:9). And the new man is everything that we are in Jesus Christ (Romans 5:19; Ephesians 4:22-24; Colossians 3:10).

From the following verses, list the characteristics of those who are God's children (saved) and those who are Adam's children (unsaved).

GOD'S CHILDREN	ADAM'S CHILDREN
1 Corinthians 15:22	1 Corinthians 15:22
Romans 6:11	Ephesians 2:1
Colossians 1:21-22	Ephesians 2:2
2 Peter 1:4	Romans 5:10
Romans 6:18	Romans 6:17
2 Corinthians 5:21	John 3:18
1 John 3:10	1 John 3:10

LIFE IN GOD'S FAMILY

When you were born again, you inherited eternal life (1 John 4:15), and God's seed was planted within you as a portion of that inheritance (1 John 3:9). The Bible also points out that you were re-created into a brand new person on the inside (2 Corinthians 5:17). At your spiritual rebirth, you were not given a new body or mind, but you were given a new nature with the promise of a glorified body still to come. This new nature allows you to live in union with Jesus Christ (Colossians 2:6-7).

According to 1 Corinthians 15:49, whose image will we bear if we are born again?

Your new life in Christ is a lifelong process of change. Although you are given a new nature, you are still in a constant battle with your old one. The reality of the Christian life is that you are an entirely new spiritual being in Christ, with a new standing before God and freedom from the tyranny of sin, but you still battle the old nature that you inherited from Adam (Galatians 5:17). The new birth does not remove the desire to sin from your life (Romans 7:22-25).

In Romans 7:15-25, what did Paul recognize about the struggle between the old, sinful nature and the new, spiritual nature?

The Apostle Paul challenges us to be renewed day by day (2 Corinthians 4:16). This implies a daily, conscious effort to strengthen yourself inwardly. The final transformation of our life in Christ will take place not on this earth, but in Heaven, when we receive our new bodies (Philippians 3:20-21; Colossians 3:4).

What is the event at which you will finally receive your glorified body (Colossians 3:4)?

According to the following verses, what are the spiritual benefits reserved exclusively for those who are members of God's family?

REFERENCE	SPIRITUAL BENEFITS
Romans 3:24	
Romans 8:1	
Romans 8:2	
1 Corinthians 1:2	
1 Corinthians 1:30	
1 Corinthians 15:22	
2 Corinthians 5:17	
2 Corinthians 5:21	
Galatians 3:28	
Ephesians 1:3	
Ephesians 1:4	
Ephesians 1:5-6	
Ephesians 1:7	
Ephesians 1:10-11	
Ephesians 1:13	
Ephesians 2:6	
Ephesians 2:10	
Ephesians 2:13	
Ephesians 3:6	
Ephesians 3:12	
Ephesians 5:29-30	
Colossians 2:10	
Colossians 2:11	

What have been some of the more significant changes in your life that have come as a result of your spiritual rebirth?

How do you respond to the author's statement in the introduction—"we have not initiated our relationship with God" (see: John 6: 37, 44-45)?

How would you describe the phrase *"born again"* to a non-believer? What passage in the Bible explains this somewhat difficult concept?

What are the five spiritual benefits that a person receives as a result of the new birth?

What two forces are at work, bringing about a spiritual rebirth? Can you explain how these two forces operate?

When you became a Christian, were the instincts and desires of your old nature completely removed? What weapons are at your disposal to help you fight against the sinful nature?

What spiritual benefits derived from being a member of God's family are especially important to you? How have they changed your whole outlook on the Christian life?

SESSION TWO

THE ASSURANCE OF SALVATION AND ETERNAL LIFE

Memory Verse: 1 John 5:13

Doubts and questions regarding the assurance of your salvation have probably surfaced many times since you were born into the family of God. It is not uncommon for new Christians and even those who have been saved for many years to experience a state of uncertainty about their eternal destiny. However, God does not intend for you to live with insecurities regarding your salvation. The Bible clearly indicates that God wants all of His children to know that they can have complete confidence in their salvation. Doubts and questions should never leave you disoriented in regards to your eternal life (Romans 8:38-39).

Even as we doubt our salvation and its security, a collective work is taking place on our behalf. The combined efforts of the Trinity are cooperating to assure us of salvation, and to give us the certainty that we are forever anchored to God. The Godhead is unchanging (Malachi 3:6), and their promise of eternal life is secure, not based in your work on their behalf, but in Their work on yours (1 Peter 1:3-5).

But how can you know for sure that you have eternal life? What are the promises that you can depend on when doubts arise regarding your eternal destiny? Can your salvation ever be "lost?"

THE WILL OF THE FATHER

The Bible gives us the confidence we need to have regarding eternal life (John 20:31). You can be sure that the promise of eternal life given to all who believe is never annulled or retracted. And this assuredness is available because the Source of your eternal life is God (John 6:39-40). God would cease to be God if He inadvertently voided an oath that He made with you.

God wants all men to share in the gift of eternal life that was made available through His Son's redemptive work on the cross (2 Peter 3:9). And He has personally promised, through an oath, eternal life to all who believe (Hebrews 6:17-18). This oath was made for our encouragement and inspiration. Our salvation is eternal because its Keeper is God (Jude 24; Psalm 121:4-7). And the power to keep is God's alone (Psalm 97:10). It rests with Him and not us (Philippians 1:6).

Read 1 John 5:11-13 and answer the following questions:

• Who has given you eternal life?

• Through whom do you receive eternal life?

• According to verse 12, is there any reason to believe that if you are saved you can lose your salvation? Who does not have eternal life according to this verse?

• What was John's reason for writing the verses that you just read (verse 13)?

- According to John 5:23-24, what is the only possible way to inherit eternal life? If you believe on the Father through the Son, will you ever face condemnation?

- What was Job looking forward to after his death (Job 19:25-27)?

THE WORK OF THE SON

Jesus Christ is the hope of our salvation (1 Timothy 1:1). It is His work as our High Priest that keeps us anchored to God (Hebrews 6:19-20). He alone is the One who keeps us from drifting away from God. As believers, our eternal destinies are anchored within the heavenly holy of holies, and Jesus Himself is the Guardian of our souls. Therefore in God's mind, our souls are already secured within the veil, behind the curtain, through the work of Jesus Christ, our eternal High Priest who is seated at God's right hand (Hebrews 1:3). The security of the hope that we have in Christ is almost unfathomable, but it was made possible by the sacrifice that Jesus made on the cross. We are forever secure through the will of the Father and the intercessory work of our great High Priest—Jesus Christ.

According to Hebrews 7:25, what is one of the functions that Christ performs on our behalf? To what extent is Christ able to save you according to this verse?

Do you think that Christ anticipated His role as High Priest when you read His prayer in John 17:11? What was He asking His Father to do?

Who was Jesus praying for in John 17:20? Do you think that you are a part of this group that Jesus was praying for?

THE WITNESS OF THE SPIRIT

In His goodness, God pledges the presence of the Third Person of the Trinity, the Holy Spirit, to every believer (Ephesians 1:13-14). This is one of the ways that God has seen fit to guarantee His promise of eternal life. The Holy Spirit is the pledge of our future inheritance. He is the first part of God's guarantee that our inheritance is secure in Heaven (1 Peter 1:4).

When you became a Christian, the Holy Spirit took up residence in your life (1 Corinthians 6:19). He is your comforter, your helper, and your advocate before God. He also empowers and equips you for ministry and service. But perhaps His most important function is assuring you of your inheritance in Jesus Christ. Your assurance must rest in the continuing work of the Holy Spirit in your life, never on the basis of a past experience.

How does Romans 8:9 describe someone who does not belong to Christ?

According to Romans 8:16-17, how do you know that you are one of God's children? What are God's children described as in verse 17?

According to Ephesians 1:13-14, who was given to you, following your salvation, as a seal of your inheritance?

According to 1 John 4:13, who lives in you as a result of your union with Christ?

Through the will of the Father, the work of the Son, and the witness of the Holy Spirit, we have confidence and assurance that our salvation is secure. When we are fully convinced of the promises and provision of God, we will no longer doubt the permanence or security of the promise of eternal life.

Read John 10:28-29. What can separate you from your relationship to God?

According to Romans 8:35-39, is there anything that can separate you from God's love?

• **What are you described as in verse 37?**

• **What does our salvation make us conquerors over?**

What does the Prophet Isaiah tell us that the effect of righteousness will produce (Isaiah 32:17)?

Do you have any doubts about the assurance of your salvation?

❏ **Yes, I am still concerned that I might lose my salvation.**

❏ **No, I feel confident in the promises and provision of God for salvation.**

DISCUSSION QUESTIONS

SESSION TWO

Why do you think Christians often doubt their salvation? Through whose collective work is our salvation secure?

Who is the source of eternal life? How has God confirmed His promise of eternal life according to Hebrews 6:17-18? Will God always keep His promise (Hebrews 6:13-15; 7:21)?

What can we learn about God's protection in Psalm 121:4-7? Do you think this protection includes His promise of eternal life for those who believe?

Through what office does Jesus Christ work as the Guardian of our souls? Can you explain this truth using Hebrews 6:19-20?

What Person of the Godhead is given to us as the first part of God's guarantee that our inheritance is eternally secure in Heaven? When do we receive His presence?

Is eternal security something that we work to obtain after we're saved? How do we know beyond a shadow of a doubt that we are forever secure?

What verses and promises can you claim when you are doubting your salvation? What is the most important truth that you learned as a result of studying this lesson?

3

THE FIRST STEP OF OBEDIENCE

Memory Verse: Romans 6:4

The first step of obedience in the life of any committed follower of Christ is baptism. The Bible mandates that baptism follow repentance (Matthew 28:19; Acts 2:37-38). Baptism is an outward display (testimony) of a life surrendered in obedience to the One who saved you. Because of this, baptism is always preceded by repentance and faith (Acts 20:21). Baptism is also a means of identification with the body of Christ—His church. In fact, the first Christians were persecuted for their willingness to publicly identify with Jesus Christ and those who followed Him. Nevertheless, baptism was an essential component in the life of the early church, and it was something that was regularly obeyed (Acts 2:38, 41; 8:12, 36-39; 9:18; 10:47; 16:15, 33; 18:8; 22:16).

At Pentecost, Peter's sermon addressed the importance of baptism. What did baptism follow (Acts 2:37-38)?

According to Acts 18:8, what was the first step taken after the Corinthians believed?

What was the prerequisite for baptism in the story of the Ethiopian eunuch found in Acts 8:36-37? What was the eunuch's testimony?

Read Matthew 28:18-20 (the Great Commission). Is baptism an essential component of the Great Commission?

• Why do you think that Jesus would leave us with the command to baptize those who became His disciples?

• According to verse 19, we are to be baptized and to baptize others in the name of whom? How does this support the doctrine of the Trinity?

THE METHOD OF BAPTISM

The first Christians identified themselves with Christ through water baptism. This act of obedience to Christ's command was always done by immersion (literally being covered with water). Pouring or sprinkling of water, which is common today, was not the method of baptism found anywhere in Scripture. (Sprinkling gained widespread acceptance in about the thirteenth century.)

We also know from careful study of the baptisms found in Scripture that there is no reference to sprinkling (Matthew 3:16; John 3:23; Acts 8:38-39). In fact, had sprinkling been the method of baptism used in the New Testament, the Holy Spirit of God would have prompted the biblical writers to use a different word. Throughout the Bible, the word *baptism* implies immersion in water.

Based on what you read in Matthew 3:16, do you think Jesus was baptized by immersion? What clues are given to reveal that Jesus was baptized by immersion?

Another indication that baptism is to be done by immersion can be found by understanding the symbolism of baptism. Baptism symbolizes the death, burial, and resurrection of Jesus Christ. A person cannot be properly buried by simply having a few shovels of dirt poured over their heads. Burial always signifies a complete and total covering of the body. So baptism, to be carried out biblically, requires full immersion of the body in water.

According to Colossians 2:12 and Romans 6:4-5, what is baptism symbolic of?

THE IMPORTANCE OF BAPTISM

While baptism is not essential for salvation (Ephesians 2:8-9), it is an indication of your heartfelt obedience to the commands of Christ and Scripture. It is only the first step of obedience to Christ in the life of a believer, but it is a vital one, because through baptism, you identify yourself with the person and cause of Jesus Christ. You are making a statement of surrender to the claims of Christ on your life.

Although baptism symbolizes the death, burial, and resurrection of Christ, it also portrays the death and burial of our old way of life, followed by the resurrection to our new life in Christ (Galatians 3:26-27; Colossians 2:12).

Baptism is an essential step towards serving in the church and growing in Christ. It is an outward display of an inner-life submission to Jesus Christ as Lord of your life, as well as the first step of obedience in the life of any disciple of Christ.

Have you taken the first step of obedience and followed Christ in believer's baptism?

❑ **Yes**

❑ **No, but I am ready to take that first step of obedience.**

DISCUSSION QUESTIONS

SESSION THREE

Why is baptism such an important first step in the life of a new believer? What is baptism always preceded by?

Would your decision to be baptized have been different if you were threatened with bodily harm, maybe even death? What gave the believers of the early church such strength and courage to take this important first step?

Why is sprinkling not a suitable method for baptism? What is the only method of baptism found in Scripture?

How would you defend your belief of baptism by immersion? What passages of Scripture would you use to support your convictions?

If a new Christian who was considering baptism approached you, what reasons would you give him to take the first step of obedience?

What is baptism symbolic of? Explain.

Is baptism necessary to be saved? Why not?

4

THE RELATIONSHIP THAT MATTERS MOST

Memory Verse: Deuteronomy 6:5

Your life as a follower of Christ is one that is to be centered and focused on God. Cultivating an intimate relationship with Him should be the divine priority of your spiritual journey. This relationship may be defined in a myriad of terms, but it always comes down to worshipping the true and living God with all of your heart, soul, mind, and strength (Deuteronomy 6:5; Mark 12:30). This involves a daily encounter with God through such disciplines as prayer, Scripture reading, and studying the Bible. God alone is worthy of worship and adoration, and He expects you to give praise only to Him (Exodus 34:14). He eagerly awaits communion with you.

What is the first commandment Jesus gave (Mark 12:30)? What is the second (Mark 12:31)?

When you find yourself in a love relationship with God, you will find that your service to others will flow directly out of your intimacy with Him. It is natural for you to love and serve others when your life has been fully surrendered to adoring the Creator of the Universe. Service flows out of worship. When service takes priority over worship, it becomes idolatry. God seeks worshippers first and foremost, and He anticipates all who are followers of His Son to be worshippers of Him (John 4:23-24). Worship is simply your response to God's initiative of seeking and drawing you to Himself (John 6:44).

What was the primary function of the Levitical priests according to Ezekiel 44:15-16?

Who has been given the responsibility to minister to God in the New Testament (1 Peter 2:5, 9; Revelation 1:6)?

According to Hebrews 13:15, what sacrifice should be offered to God? How is this different from the sacrificial system of the Old Testament (Hebrews 13:11)?

THE PRIORITY OF A LIFETIME

The Bible reveals that a good portion of our eternal existence with God will be spent in worship of Him (Revelation 5:9-14). In Heaven, we will be in a state of perpetual praise and worship of God for who He is and what He has done. Therefore, growth as a worshipper is the divine priority of our spiritual life. And growth is only obtainable when worship develops as a way of life. We are to give God a continuous sacrifice of praise and thanksgiving for all that He has done on our behalf (Psalm 100:4-5). No other person is worthy of the worship and adoration that belongs to God.

What was Peter's response when Cornelius attempted to worship Him (Acts 10:25-26)?

According to Acts 14:11-15, how did Barnabas and Paul respond to being worshiped by the people of Lystra?

In Revelation 19:10, what was the angel's response to being worshiped by John (the writer of Revelation)?

Why do you think that godly men and angels refused to accept worship that was given to them?

What was Jesus' response to being worshiped (Matthew 8:2-4)?

DEEPENING THE RELATIONSHIP

Your relationship with God and its potential for growth and development is only limited by your passion to expand and experience it. God will never close the door to those who are pursuing Him with pure hearts (Psalm 24:4-5). He is looking for true worshippers (John 4:23), those that are committed and devoted to knowing Him (Colossians 1:10), fellowshipping with Him, praising Him (Psalm 50:23), and experiencing Him through the journey of life.

Worshipping God is not a technique, but a lifestyle. The following biblical insights will help you develop the relationship that matters most:

• **Develop a spiritual thirst for God** (Psalm 42:1-2; 63:1). You will grow in direct proportion to your intake of spiritual things. So to develop a thirst for God, you will have to deepen your understanding of Him. This happens through the experiences of life and the illumination of the Holy Spirit.

What was the one desire of David's life according to Psalm 27:4?

• **Develop an exalted view of God** (Isaiah 6:1-7). Do not allow yourself to be deceived into thinking that God is nothing more than "the man upstairs." Whenever someone encountered God in the Bible, he was overtaken with fear and trepidation (Exodus 3:5-6; Luke 7:16). God's holiness and righteousness are not to be ignored nor forgotten.

According to Psalm 46:10, what does God want from you?

• **Develop a heart of gratitude for God's goodness** (Psalm 100:4-5; Luke 7:41-47). The Bible tells us to give thanks in everything that we do (1 Thessalonians 5:18). This includes worshipping God with a thankful heart and a spirit of gratitude. God is the source and provider of all that we have (Psalm 62:1), and He is worthy of our thanks and gratitude. We should come before Him with an offering of thanksgiving and a sacrifice of praise.

How often does Paul admonish the church at Ephesus to thank God (Ephesians 5:20)?

• **Develop a passion for prayer** (Psalm 27:8). God listens to the prayers of His people (Psalm 34:4). He speaks to us through these times of communication with Him, and He reveals Himself to us in wonderful ways (Jeremiah 33:3). God is moved by the prayers of those He loves (James 5:16), and He longs for us to commune with Him intimately through the channel of prayer (Psalm 27:4; 62:8). Worship, adoration, thanksgiving, confession, and supplication are all expressed through the prayers of God's people. Prayer is your lifeline to God—your spiritual power supply.

As Christians, how should we approach the throne of grace (Hebrews 4:16)? Who makes this possible (Hebrews 4:14-15)?

DISCUSSION QUESTIONS

SESSION FOUR

Why is your relationship with God the most important priority of your spiritual life? What distractions can stand in the way of developing a more intimate relationship with Him?

What happens when we allow our ministry or service to take priority over our worship of God? Why is this unhealthy for us spiritually?

Do you believe that it is every believer's responsibility to worship God? What happens when believers willfully neglect their relationship with God?

In what ways do we worship God individually? In what ways does the church worship God?

Is worshipping God a technique or a way of life? How would you explain this worshipping lifestyle to a new believer?

Of the four biblical insights that the author gave to help you develop the relationship that matters most, which one really challenged you? In what area were you the strongest? The weakest?

Why is prayer such an important aspect of our relationship with God? How does the author describe prayer at the end of this lesson? Do you agree?

THE ENEMY EXPOSED

Memory Verse: 1 Peter 5:8

The greatest enemy that the Christian has is Satan. (*Satan* means "enemy" or "adversary.") He is deceitful, subtle, cunning, and entirely wicked. He wants nothing more than to see the cause of Christ defeated. He is the ruler and prince of this world (John 12:31; Ephesians 2:2) and controls and influences the system of values and morals that the world endorses. His attack on Christians comes from all sides, and He would love to see committed followers of Christ given over to the desires and cravings of the flesh. To not take his influence seriously is a huge error in judgment.

Take a moment to read the following Scriptures and write down how Satan is described in each verse:

REFERENCE	DESCRIPTION OF SATAN
1 Peter 5:8	
1 Thessalonians 3:5	
Matthew 13:19	
John 8:44	
John 16:11	
2 Corinthians 4:4	
2 Corinthians 11:14	
1 John 2:13	
Revelation 12:9	
Revelation 12:10	

Satan does his work by casting doubt on what God says (Genesis 3:1). This was his original plan, and the one by which he still operates quite successfully today. He also oppresses people physically, mentally, and spiritually (Acts 10:38) and intends to leave everyone and everything in his path in ruin (Luke 22:31).

What is Paul's warning to the church in Ephesus concerning the devil (Ephesians 4:27)? What do you think Paul means?

What should be your strategy to get rid of Satan (James 4:7)? What do you think this means?

THE BATTLEGROUND

Gaining ground in the Christian life is a constant battle between your two natures—the old and the new. You may have encountered this struggle already between the desire to do right (the spiritual nature; the "spirit") and the constant temptation to do wrong (the carnal nature; the "flesh") (Galatians 5:17). The Apostle Paul concluded that the battle could only be won through the strength of the Lord Jesus Christ (Romans 7:15-25).

Your old nature was inherited at birth from Adam (Romans 5:12). It includes the desire to indulge the flesh and the mind (Ephesians 2:3). It is hostile towards God and has no desire to please Him (Romans 8:7-8), and the Bible tells us that nothing good can come from it (Romans 7:18). God's Word is also clear that a continuous pattern of indulging the passions of the old nature is a mark of someone who will not inherit the kingdom of God (Galatians 5:21).

What is the old nature called in the following verses?

• **Ephesians 4:22:**

• **Colossians 3:9:**

• **Romans 8:7:**

When we are saved, we are given a new nature (2 Peter 1:4). It is vital that the new nature gain victory over the old one. And the only way to do this is to draw on the power available through the Holy Spirit living in us (Acts 1:8); to nourish the new nature through the Word of God; and to starve the old nature by not indulging its desires and instincts. This will require patience, dedication, and trust in the provision and promises of God, as well as suiting up in the spiritual armor available to every believer (Ephesians 6:11-18).

What are the pieces of spiritual armor found in Ephesians 6:11-18?

Side by side, list out the vices of the old nature and the virtues of the new nature found in Galatians 5.

VICES OF THE OLD NATURE Galatians 5:19-21	VIRTUES OF THE NEW NATURE Galatians 5:22-23

What is the new nature called in the following verses?

• **2 Corinthians 5:17:**

• **Ephesians 4:24:**

What was Paul's strategy for defeating the old nature (1 Corinthians 9:27)?

THE STRATEGY

Satan's strategy has always been to assault our old nature on three fronts (1 John 2:16). His plan is simple and effective. First, he intends to entice our flesh. Second, he will attempt to control our vision. And third, Satan always appeals to our pride. Consider the following examples:

Read Genesis 3:1-6. What is the three-fold pattern of deception that Satan used to deceive Eve according to verse 6?

1.

2.

3.

Read Matthew 4:1-11. Even with Jesus, what did Satan try to appeal to when he tempted Him?

1. (verses 2-3)

2. (verses 5-6)

3. (verses 8-9)

How did Jesus counter Satan's temptation in Matthew 4: 4, 7, 10?

What is one of the weapons at your disposal to resist Satan's strategy (Ephesians 6:17)?

Satan's strategy to conquer and defeat humanity has been in operation since creation. He intends to defeat us through the influence of the world and the manipulation of the flesh. But Satan also knows that God has given us four resources to meet the enemy head on. Satan's only hope is that we don't take advantage of the arsenal of our faith.

- The indwelling Holy Spirit (Romans 8:9-13)
- The interceding of our great High Priest (Hebrews 7:25)
- The Word of God (Ephesians 6:17; Hebrews 4:12; Colossians 3:16)
- The power of prayer (Hebrews 4:16)

THE VICTORY

You can take great confidence in the fact that Jesus Christ has already conquered every temptation that you face. Every enticement that draws you has a way of escape (1 Corinthians 10:13). You do not have to live a defeated Christian life. You are under no obligation to the world, the flesh, or the devil (Romans 8:12).

We have been guaranteed the victory to overcome the debilitating disease of sin through the power of the Spirit according to the Apostle Paul (Romans 8:9). As Christ followers, Satan no longer has authority over our lives, unless we submit to His control. And through Christ's work on our behalf, provision has been made for our victory over Satan and all of his vices. Consider the defeat that Satan was dealt when Jesus was victorious over death and the grave:

- Satan was defeated (John 12:31; John 16:11).
- Satan's power over Christians was broken (Colossians 2:15; Hebrews 2:14).
- The influence of the world was overcome (John 16:33; 1 John 5:4).
- The power of the flesh was destroyed (Romans 8:3).
- Christians are no longer slaves to sin (Romans 6:14, 20-22).

Spiritual warfare is inevitable, but we can enter the battle with complete confidence in the outcome. Christ came to destroy the works of Satan (1 John 3:8), and He was successful in His mission. Satan already knows his final resting place (Revelation 20:1-3, 10), but until that moment when he is bound and thrown into his place of eternal torment, we must be vigilant and aware that he is out to destroy us, always resting in the strength and power of God to lead us to victory.

DISCUSSION QUESTIONS

SESSION FIVE

What does *Satan* mean? Should his influence and power be taken seriously? Why?

What has and always will be Satan's plan? Who were the first people to encounter this plan in action? What was the outcome?

How would you describe the "battleground" of the Christian life? Are Christians exempt from the ongoing tension of doing what is right and the constant temptation to do wrong? Explain this inner battle.

What three ways does the author provide to help the new nature gain victory over the old one? Can victory ever be obtained without the indwelling Holy Spirit?

What additional weapons does God graciously provide for the spiritual war (Ephesians 6:11-18)? Which of these weapons are offensive? Which are defensive? Why are both necessary?

Satan's strategy always includes direct assaults in three areas of our lives. What are they? Did his strategy change during the temptation of Jesus? Why was Jesus' defensive strategy so effective (Matthew 4:4, 7, 10)?

What is the promise of 1 Corinthians 10:13? Why is this verse such a wonderful promise when faced with the temptation to sin? How can being active with other followers of Christ help you during times of temptation?

THE ADVENTURE OF MAKING DISCIPLES

Memory Verse: Matthew 28:19-20

When you became a child of God, you were given a new mission for your life (Matthew 28:19-20)—a mission that includes the opportunity to share with others the abundant life that is available to them through a personal relationship with Jesus Christ (John 10:10). We all encounter hundreds of people a week who are far from God and need to be in a relationship with Him. God has placed us in the jobs where we work, in the neighborhoods where we live, and in the restaurants where we eat for a specific reason—He wants us to share the light.

How can we be a non-stop witness for Christ, according to Matthew 5:16?

What is the word *light* referring to? Use 1 Peter 2:12 to find your answer.

What three instructions are given in Jesus' Great Commission (Matthew 28:18-20)?

1.

2.

3.

According to Acts 4:12, who is salvation found in?

According to Mark 8:38, what are the consequences of rejecting Christ?

KNOWING WHAT TO SAY

Sharing Christ with another person should never be something that we fear. It should be the natural outgrowth of our love for God and that person. The Bible tells us to be prepared to share the Good News of what Christ has done for us (1 Peter 3:15-16). This is done most effectively during the normal activities of our daily lives.

What is the basic message of the Gospel found in John 3:16?

What is the evangelism approach that Peter recommends (1 Peter 3:15-16)? With what attitude are we to give our answer?

What were the main points of Paul's evangelism outline (1 Corinthians 15:1-8)? Why do you think Paul included his personal testimony (verse 8)?

Your personal testimony is an essential element of the evangelism process. Have you ever developed a concise, personal testimony (4-6 minutes in length) of being born again? Write the highlights of your testimony in the space provided below.

THE REST OF THE STORY

Going out and sharing the Good News is only one part of the Great Commission. Jesus left us with additional responsibilities. He told us to go out and make disciples (this is the process of evangelism), but it didn't end there. He also commanded us to baptize and teach the new disciples (this is the process of disciplemaking). To be completely obedient to the Great Commission, we must be involved in evangelism and discipleship, reaching and equipping, sharing and teaching. This involves a relationship. We have a responsibility to invest in the lives of others in ongoing disciplemaking relationships.

What were the key points to Paul's challenge to Timothy in 2 Timothy 2:22? Did Paul expect Timothy to flee his fleshly instincts alone?

What was the discipleship process that Paul gave to Timothy (2 Timothy 2:2)? How many "generations" of disciples are represented?

What four things did Paul ask the church to begin doing in Philippians 4:9?

SESSION SIX

What new mission were you given when you became a Christian? Under whose authority have we been commissioned to make disciples? Are there any limits to this authority?

In what practical ways can you fulfill the Great Commission in your family? Your job? Your neighborhood? Your leisure activities?

Within the context of your present relationships (i.e. family, friends, coworkers, etc....), develop a list of five people that you know who are not saved. Pray for an opportunity to reach these people and share the Good News.

Why is your personal testimony such a powerful aspect of your evangelistic efforts? How does your faith story break down the defenses of someone who doesn't want to hear about God?

Practically speaking, why is discipleship such an important element of the Great Commission? Can you obey all of the Great Commission while neglecting the critical process of discipleship? Why not?

How would you describe the Great Commission lifestyle to a brand new believer? What Scriptures would you use to promote this new way of living?

On a scale of 1 to 10, how effective have you been at making disciples? What steps will you take to improve your mission effectiveness?

How all-encompassing was Paul's approach to discipleship according to Philippians 4:9? Did his discipleship process just include going through a course or curriculum? Why not?

4 THE CHURCH: BECOMING A PART OF GOD'S PLAN

INTRODUCTION

The church is God's idea. He is the Master Architect in a project that is still under construction (Matthew 16:18; Acts 15:14-18). Now He employs us—His construction
crew—to build upon the foundation that millions of Christians over the past two thousand
years have given their lives and their resources to construct (Acts 2:44-45; 4:32; 7:54-60).
And the sheer size of the assignment cannot be underestimated. We have been challenged
and commanded to go out and make disciples of everyone (Matthew 28:18-20). This is
not something that can be done individually by one person or one church. It requires the
collective effort of thousands of churches and millions of Christians all around the world.

When God decided that the best way to make disciples was to penetrate communities, villages, towns, and cities all over the globe with a nucleus of committed Christ followers
that He would call the church, He did this out of divine foresight. He understood that we
would be unable to effectively make disciples on our own. We need the support, encouragement, accountability, training, and relationships that the church provides. God knew
that in order for us to effectively go out into the world, we would have to regularly come
in to the loving and nurturing support of His family (Hebrews 10:25). Being God's
ambassadors (2 Corinthians 5:20) to the world requires frequent reminders that this world
is not our home. We are citizens of God's kingdom (Ephesians 2:19) and members of His
household. The gathered community of believers provides us with a taste of that future
hope (Colossians 1:5).

The church, in all its variety, has been designed by God to carry out the ministry of reconciliation that Jesus Christ began (2 Corinthians 5:18-19). We have no greater
responsibility, no higher calling, than to be revealers of Christ to spiritually lost people.
We are in the world for the sake of those who need to be brought into a relationship with
God. And the church shines most brightly when its members understand their personal
responsibility to be salt and light (Matthew 5:13-14). But too often the church has come to
be a place for spectators. Rather it is to be a band of authentic disciples, bound together
by the Holy Spirit and committed to bringing glory to God.

A church that is clear on its purpose and undistracted by its critics is the hope of a spiritually lost world, because God has made it His personal project to build His church and
nothing will stop its progress. Can you think of anything more worthy of investing your
time, your spiritual gifts, and your God-given resources?

WHAT IS THE CHURCH (PART 1)?

Memory Verse: Matthew 16:18

Defining the church is a task of truly biblical proportions. It may be just as important to understand what the church is not before we begin to explore what it is.

- **The church is not a physical building.** The building—the structure—is simply a place for the church to gather. Its ornamentation, architecture, or steeple does not make it a church. It is important to know that all throughout the New Testament the word *church* is never used to describe a building. When a person understands the church as just a building, the phrase most often heard is, *"We attend the church on the corner of Main Street and Broad Street."*

- **The church is not an institution or organization.** These flawed concepts have developed without any reference to the biblical understanding of a church. When the church is understood in this way, the statement most often made is, *"We belong to the Roman Catholic, Methodist, or Baptist church."*

- **The church is not a series of services or activities that happen throughout the week.** These are simply the functions that the gathered community of believers use as a means to achieve a desired end. If the church is defined as services and activities, you will often hear, *"We go to church on Sundays"* or *"We've always been active in church."*

Many times you will also hear the church defined as a "congregation," but even this definition loses the real meaning of the word *church*. A congregation is simply a group of people who have gathered together. *A church is a group of people who have been called out to gather together.* This definition places all of the emphasis on the work and action of God.

In its purest biblical form, the church, according to William Barclay, *"is a body of people, not so much assembling because they have chosen to come together but assembling because God has called them to himself; not so much assembling to share their own thoughts and opinions, but assembling to listen to the voice of God."*[1]

The New Testament uses the word *church* in four distinctive ways:

1. The word *church* refers to the universal Church (1 Corinthians 10:32; 12:28; Philippians 3:6)—also known in Scripture as the *"church of God"* (1 Corinthians 1:2; 2 Corinthians 1:1). The universal church is made up of all believers on earth at any given time.

2. The word *church* refers to a particular local church (Romans 16:1; Galatians 1:2; 1 Thessalonians 1:1). The New Testament places the most emphasis on the church in its local setting.

3. The word *church* refers to the actual gathering of believers in any place for worship (1 Corinthians 11:18; 14:19, 23).

4. The word *church* refers to the body of Christ (Colossians 1:24) with Christ as the head (Ephesians 5:23-24). It is through the church that Christ does His work. As His followers, we are Christ's hands, feet, and voice.

Which of the following verses describe the church expressed universally and which describe the church expressed in its local form?

• **Colossians 1:18** _____   • **1 Thessalonians 1:1** _____

• **Galatians 1:1-2** _____   • **Ephesians 5:25** _____

In the first century, the Lord added to the local fellowship of believers all those who were being saved (Acts 2:47). This fellowship or gathering was known as the *ekklesia*—translated in English as "church." It was this local body of believers that experienced the outpouring of the Holy Spirit (Acts 4:31). Through the Holy Spirit's empowerment and the intense persecution that they faced, the church spread throughout the civilized world. God's big idea was working through His unique group (Titus 2:14; 1 Peter 2:9) of "called out ones"—the Church.

How does the Apostle Paul describe the church in 1 Timothy 3:15? What "truth" do you think the church is to strengthen and support? In what book is this "truth" found?

Why would it be difficult to fulfill the following biblical commands if you were not actively involved in the life of the church?

• **Proverbs 27:17**

• **Galatians 6:1-3**

• **Colossians 3:16**

According to 1 Peter 2:9, what are the four descriptive designations given to the church?

1.

2.

3.

4.

In your own words, how would you describe the church if someone were to ask you?

You can understand the church best by recognizing its dual responsibility—its two-fold identity. The church is a people who have been both called out of the world to glorify God and sent back into the world to make disciples. We are called out to be a holy people, but to live out that holiness before a watching world that desperately needs to be reconciled to God. Jesus Christ gave us the greatest example of this kind of life, but we must remember that to enter into the darkened world around us should never be done at the expense of our own Christian integrity. We are called to uphold the values of Jesus Christ in every area of our lives.

DISCUSSION QUESTIONS

SESSION ONE

Who is ultimately responsible for building the church? Why do you think the author used the term "construction crew" to describe the church's members? Would "subcontractors" have been a better description? Why or why not?

Would you describe the majority of your involvement in the church as spectator or participant? Why?

What "ministry," given in 2 Corinthians 5:18-19, was the church designed to accomplish? Why is this such an important responsibility?

What are some of the reasons why the "church" is so misunderstood? How do the majority of people describe the church? How did you view the church before you became a Christian?

What is the definition given for the word *church*? Within the context of this definition, what are the main differences between a congregation and a church?

What was the Greek word used in the New Testament that translated into our English word *church*? How did the first century *ekklesia* spread so rapidly?

How would you describe the church's dual responsibility—its two-fold identity? Do these objectives seem to conflict? Why or why not?

What is the most compelling reason to be an active participant, a vital contributor to the local church?

WHAT IS THE CHURCH (PART 2)?

Memory Verse: Romans 12:5

THE CHURCH IS A BODY

The single most important metaphor for the church is seen when the Bible describes the church as a body (Romans 12:5) with Christ functioning as the Head (Ephesians 5:23). This vivid picture of the church as a single unit captures the heart of Jesus' own prayer in the Gospel of John for the church to be one (John 17:11-23). Unity of the body was what Jesus envisioned for the church, and as Christ's body, the church exists exclusively to do

Christ's will and to be His presence in the world. He never intended for the church to function as independent parts, but as a unified whole—one body with many parts.

But what does the church body look like when it is functioning the way God intended?

1. The church body is *unified* (Ephesians 4:3-6). The church, even with its diversity of parts, is to be one. God's plan is for the church to be free of all division in its local setting. Our responsibility is to maintain the highest level of spiritual unity possible (Ephesians 4:3) and to avoid anyone or anything that causes division in the local fellowship (1 Corinthians 1:10; 12:24-25; Titus 3:10-11).

2. The church body is *diverse* (1 Corinthians 12:12-14). Each member is making a unique contribution for the good of the whole body (Romans 12:4-8). While we do not all have the same function, we are to share in the same goal. Just as each part of the human body is important to the well being of the body as a whole, so each member of the church is critical to the overall health of the church body. Each one of us brings differing gifts and talents that allow the church to function as God planned.

3. The church body is *interdependent* (1 Corinthians 12:20-24). The truth is that we need each other. God did not make us to function as a group of disconnected parts, but as a unified whole. At the moment of our new birth, God wired us up to function and serve as contributing members of the local church. He gave us irreplaceable gifts and talents that are designed to serve and build up the local body of Christ.

According to Colossians 1:18 and Ephesians 5:23, who is the head, or leader, of the church?

What is the church described as in Ephesians 1:22-23? Who made Christ the Head of the church according to verse 22?

Read Romans 12:4-8 and 1 Corinthians 12:12-27. What is the central point that the Apostle Paul is trying to make in these passages?

THE CHURCH IS A FLOCK

The Bible paints a wonderful picture of the church as the flock of God. This image carries with it a wonderful sense of the protection and provision of the Chief Shepherd—Jesus Christ— (1Peter 5:4) as He graciously leads and guides His flock, the church. The Shepherd knows what is best for His sheep, and His sheep hear His voice and respond to His leadership (John 10:1-5). The Bible provides numerous examples where God's people are compared to a flock of sheep with the Lord as their Shepherd (Genesis 48:15; Psalm 23; Psalm 100:3; Isaiah 53:6-7; Luke 15:3-7).

As the Chief Shepherd, Jesus has appointed "elders" (also known as shepherds; bishops; overseers; pastors) to love and care for His flock until His return (1 Peter 5:1-4; Acts 20:28). As God's flock, we can have complete confidence that we will never be separated from His watchful care, because His promise as our Shepherd is that He will never leave or forsake His sheep (Hebrews 13:5).

What are some of the responsibilities that the elders/shepherds have when caring for the flock of God (1 Peter 5:1-4)?

What do the following verses teach about the characteristics of an authentic disciple in the church?

- **1 Corinthians 16:15-16:**

- **1 Thessalonians 5:12-13:**

- **Hebrews 13:17:**

According to 1 Peter 5:2, who does the flock belong to? Who will be reunited with His flock and reward the faithful elders (1 Peter 5:4)?

Read John 21:15-17. What was the command Jesus repeatedly gave to Peter? How many times did Jesus issue this command? What was each command preceded by?

Do you think that Jesus' three-fold command to Peter in John 21 had anything to do with His promise that Peter would be instrumental in laying the foundation of the church (Matthew 16:18-19)?

DISCUSSION QUESTIONS

SESSION TWO

?

Why do you think the Bible uses the image of the body to describe the church? Why wouldn't the use of the words fingers, toes, limbs, or organs have been enough of a description?

What was Christ's prayer for the church? Why do you think the unity of the church was one of His primary concerns? In what practical ways does lack of unity hinder the advance of the Gospel?

What three qualities does the author use to describe the church body when it is functioning the way God intended?

According to Ephesians 4:2-3, what qualities promote unity in the body of Christ? How does viewing God as our Father contribute to our unity (Ephesians 4:6)?

What is the point of Paul's teaching in 1 Corinthians 12:26? Is this the normal response in your church?

How can the church actively develop a healthy "body-building" program? What "exercises" would this program include? What exercises do you think the Apostle Paul would include?

What are some of the most deadly forms of disease that can plague the body of Christ?

How has the metaphor of the church as a flock of sheep brought comfort and encouragement to you?

3

WHAT IS THE CHURCH (PART 3)?

Memory Verse: 1 Peter 2:9

THE CHURCH IS A TEMPLE

The Bible reveals that God makes His home in the church that He is in the process of building (Ephesians 2:19-22; 1 Peter 2:5). He is personally building up a place, a spiritual house, where He can dwell, and He is also making His home in us as individual members of His church (1 Corinthians 3:16-17; 6:19). We are His temple, and He dwells within us. This indwelling is accomplished by and through the work of the Holy Spirit.

When the Scriptures refer to the church as a temple, the metaphor is carried directly from the Old Testament and refers to God's earthly dwelling place in Israel (2 Chronicles 6:1-2). However, in the New Testament God's presence is no longer centered around a special building but within the fellowship of His people. Because God's presence now lies within us through His Holy Spirit, we are commanded to live holy lives (1 Corinthians 3:16-17; 6:19-20).

Read Ephesians 2:19-22 and answer the following questions:

• **As followers of Christ, who are we "fellow citizens" with (verse 19)?**

• **According to verse 20, what group of people makes up the foundation of the temple God is building?**

• **Who is the "chief cornerstone" of God's dwelling place (verse 20)?**

• **For what purpose are we being built together according to verse 22?**

• **How does God live within us (verse 22)?**

According to 1 Peter 2:5, what two words are used to describe those who belong to Jesus Christ? What are we being built up to be?

The church is the temple of God. We are God's spiritual house. He has chosen to indwell His redeemed people both individually and collectively, and He has made it abundantly clear that His dwelling place is to be holy and sacred, set apart exclusively for His use. Anyone that attempts to defile or destroy the temple of God is warned that they will be destroyed (1 Corinthians 3:17). This is a fitting reminder that God is serious about building His church, and He will not allow anything to stand in His way. Become an active participant in God's building program, so that God can use your life to draw people to Himself.

THE CHURCH IS A FAMILY

The Word of God teaches that as the church we are the "sons and daughters" of God. (2 Corinthians 6:17-18). This reference indicates our relationship together as a family, united together under the common bond of our faith in Jesus Christ (Galatians 3:26). One of the privileges of our family inheritance is the gift of the indwelling Holy Spirit (Galatians 4:6-7). Additionally, we are now urged as God's family members to call on God as our "Abba, Father." (*Abba* is the Aramaic word for "Father.") This indicates that we are now free to enjoy an intimate relationship with God, because we are His children, born into His family.

The church, both in its universal and local expressions, is the family of God, joined together as God's redemptive community to experience the indwelling Holy Spirit and the freedom of an intimate relationship with God as Father and Jesus Christ as Lord. But what is the biblical pattern of living together as a spiritual family? What are the implications of this image of the church on our lives? How do we respond to one another as the sons and daughters of God?

1. As a church family, *obedience to the Father is crucial to community life* (1 John 1:7; 5:2-3). Our obedience to the Father's commands will directly impact our relationship to the family as a whole. When the church, individually and corporately, seeks to be obedient to God, the quality of spiritual life and interpersonal relationships within the family increases dramatically.

According to 1 John 5:2, how do we know that we love the children of God? How do we show our love for God (verse 3)?

2. As a church family, *unity must be vigorously protected* (John 17:11). The most disruptive and destructive element of church life is when division and discord are common within the family of God. The Bible urges us to do good things for one another (Galatians 6:10). This biblical injunction by the Apostle Paul lies in stark contrast to a church that is plagued by a spirit of disunity.

What was the central point of Paul's message to the church of Corinth in 1 Corinthians 3:1-9? How does Paul describe those involved in causing division and fights (verse 3)? What three terms did Paul use to describe God's children in verse 9?

What was Paul's challenge to the church at Ephesus regarding unity (Ephesians 4:3)?

According to Ephesians 4:4-6, what are the seven things that God's children are one in?

1.   5.

2.   6.

3.   7.

4.

3. As a church family, *forgiveness and reconciliation should permeate every relationship* (Matthew 5:23-24; 18:15; Galatians 6:1-2). It should be normal for believers to seek out those they have offended and ask for forgiveness. Life together in God's family will require moments of being made right with another brother or sister, because until Christ's return, we cannot expect every family relationship to be free from quarreling.

Read Matthew 18:15-17. What steps of reconciliation should you take in dealing with a brother or sister who sins against you?

• **STEP 1:** _____

• **STEP 2:** _____

• **STEP 3:** _____

• **STEP 4:** _____

4. As a church family, *mutual love must exist between every family member* (Mark 12:31; Ephesians 4:15-16; 1 John 4:19-21). We are commanded in Scripture to love each other, but not in a self-seeking way (1 John 4:10). The church should be the one place, perhaps the only place, where God's children feel loved, cared for, respected, and appreciated for their unique contribution. Additionally, we should be actively challenging each family member to greater depths of love (Hebrews 10:24). Love is one virtue that cannot be cultivated alone. It is the product of active participation in the family of God. Remember, as God's children, we exist to extend God's love to everyone, but especially to those we call brothers and sisters (Galatians 6:10).

What are the two great commandments that Jesus gave in Mark 12:30-31?

COMMANDMENT #1:

COMMANDMENT #2:

Is it possible for only one of these commandments to be kept without breaking them both, according to 1 John 4:19-21? What do these verses call those who say they love God and yet hate their brother?

Why do you think that the Scriptures teach us so much about loving the family of God, not causing divisions, and seeking unity in the church?

DISCUSSION QUESTIONS

SESSION THREE

What is the primary distinction between the temple of the Old Testament and the temple described in the New Testament? How should this distinction challenge us to live more holy lives?

On which dwelling, your spiritual temple or your physical house, have you spent more time decorating, remodeling, and maintaining? Why is it so difficult for believers to live with an eternal perspective?

Would you describe your spiritual condition more as a dilapidated shed than the dwelling place of God? Can your spiritual condition improve on its own?

Why do you think such a stern warning is given in 1 Corinthians 3:17? In what ways do we destroy the temple of God?

In your opinion, why does the Bible refer to the church as a family? What implications does this description have on the way we respond to one another?

The author points out that obedience to the Father is crucial to community life. Perhaps you have seen a family that doesn't follow the leadership of the father. How would you describe that scenario?

Why does unity need to be vigorously protected? What happens when unity of the family becomes threatened?

Can the family of God be obedient to the commands of the Father while simultaneously not loving one another? Why not? What role does love play in the family of God?

WHY DOES THE CHURCH EXIST (PART 1)?

Memory Verse: 1 Corinthians 10:31

The church exists to glorify God (1 Corinthians 10:31). The Bible makes it abundantly clear that this is the primary purpose of the church (Romans 15:5-9; Ephesians 1:5-12; 3:21). In fact, if God is properly glorified within the body, the other purposes of the church will also be effectively accomplished. These additional purposes include:

• **Discipleship**—Exploring God's Way (Matthew 18:20; Ephesians 4:11-13; 1 Timothy 2:2).

• **Worship**—Exalting God's Work (John 4:23-24; Acts 2:47; Philippians 3:3).

• **Evangelism**—Expanding God's Kingdom (Matthew 28:18-20; Acts 1:8; 2 Peter 3:9).

• **Fellowship**—Encouraging God's people (Acts 2:42-47; John 13:34-35; Hebrews 10:24-25).

• **Ministry**—Extending God's grace (Matthew 25:34-40; 1 Peter 4:10-11).

There are many other activities that the church has engaged in since its inception at Pentecost (Acts 2), but all of these things are secondary to the primary purpose of the church, which is to glorify God through discipleship, worship, evangelism, fellowship, and ministry. What God has commissioned the church to do cannot be accomplished by any other group of people on earth. We have been given an extraordinary opportunity to be God's ambassadors, carrying a message to a lost world that in Christ there is freedom and forgiveness of sins (Colossians 1:14).

Read Acts 2:42-47, which describes the activities of the first believers who gathered together after Pentecost and answers the following questions:

• **What are some of the activities described in these verses? How do these activities fulfill the overall purposes of the church given above?**

• **According to these verses, what were some of the characteristic marks of these early Christians? How did their behavior impact the non-believing Jews (verse 47)?**

• **Who was solely responsible for the growth of the first century church (verse 47)?**

What does Matthew 28:18-20 reveal that the church has been called out to accomplish? What is the reassurance given to the church at the end of verse 20?

According to Acts 1:8, how far does Christ expect us to go as His "witnesses?" Who does this verse reveal as the enabling agent for this worldwide mission?

The Bible paints a clear picture of why the church exists. And within that Scriptural framework there is no evidence whatsoever to support a passive, spectator-like approach to Christianity. The very first church in Acts provides ample evidence that the family of God, indwelt by the Holy Spirit and surrendered to the leadership of Jesus Christ, is an organism of growth and not one of paralysis and decay (Acts 6:1,7; 12:24; 19:20). The church is to be a living, breathing extension of the triune God, seeking to make an impact on the world around it.

DISCIPLESHIP—EXPLORING GOD'S WAY

Growing in obedience to the teachings of Scripture and the commands of Jesus Christ is not something that happens automatically as a result of the new birth. Growth is cultivated through the ongoing process of discipleship. Someone who desires to be a disciple (i.e. student, learner, follower) of Jesus Christ understands the necessity of devoting himself or herself to the exploration of God's way as it is revealed in the Bible. This exploration is a lifelong process. It is a daily denial of the old ways of thinking, acting, and living that were normal before you were born again. Additionally, no measurable gains can be made in the Christ-life without the ongoing interpersonal relationships that are available within the local church (2 Timothy 2:22). The local church is the living, breathing body of Christ, and God has designed this group of people to be an incubator for life-change and spiritual growth.

Read Ephesians 4:11-16 and answer the following questions:

• **What are the five categories of spiritual leadership given by the Apostle Paul in verse 11?**

• **Why did Christ appoint these spiritual leaders to the church according to verse 12?**

• **What is the goal of spiritual growth supposed to be according to verse 13-14?**

• **How does the body of Christ grow according to verse 16? In what way does this verse indicate that spiritual growth is not a solitary process?**

According to 1 Timothy 2:2, what kind of "lives" are Christ's disciples supposed to live? What two spiritual virtues identify this kind of life?

DISCUSSION QUESTIONS ?

SESSION FOUR

What is the primary purpose of the church? When this purpose is ignored, what can eventually happen to a church?

What are the five sub-purposes of the church as given by the author? Do you agree with these purposes? Would you have added any others?

How did the early church in Acts effectively accomplish the primary purpose of the church while engaging in the sub-purposes?

What do you recognize to be the most remarkable characteristic of the first church in Acts 2:42-47? How does your church compare with the first gathered fellowship here?

According to the author, how is growth cultivated? Do you agree with the author that growth is a lifelong process? Why or why not?

Why are the interpersonal relationships that the church provides so important to your spiritual development? Can you grow in any significant way without these relationships?

In your mind, is discipleship the process of completing a prescribed curriculum or do you see it as a lifelong process of spiritual multiplication? What are the differences between these two views?

WHY DOES THE CHURCH EXIST (PART 2)?

Memory Verse: Acts 1:8

WORSHIP—EXALTING GOD'S WORK

Worship not only brings the church to life, but it also brings Life to the church (Psalm 22:3; John 4:23-24). The Bible tells us that it is a good thing to praise God (Psalm 147:1). If the church's primary purpose for existing is to glorify God, then it is safe to say that worship should be the focal point of church life. But what is worship? In his book, *The Worship of God*, Ralph Martin defines worship as *"the dramatic celebration of God in his supreme worth in such a manner that his 'worthiness' becomes the norm and inspiration of human living."*[2] When was the last time that God's worthiness became the inspiration for your life? According to this definition, the focus of our worship should not be on the forms or the format, although these are significant. The focus of our worship and our lives as God's sons and daughters is God Himself. He alone is worthy to be praised. The Bible teaches that we are to be a worshipping people, offering the Father the glory due only to Him.

There are two essential themes that emerge from the Bible in regards to worshipping God:

1. We are to worship God for who He is—His eternal attributes (Psalm 29:2; 96:8).
2. We are to worship God for what He does—His creating and saving work (Revelation 4:11; 5:9).

What are we to give to God in worship according to Psalm 29:2 and Psalm 96:8-9? "In" what do we worship God according to the psalmist (29:2b; 96:9a)?

What is the eternal occupation of the four creatures and the twenty-four elders mentioned in Revelation 4:6-11?

What are the different forms that King David implemented in worship (1 Chronicles 16:1-7)? List as many as possible.

Read Revelation 5:8-10. What is the central message of the song the creatures and elders sing while worshipping the Lamb (Jesus Christ)?

FIVE ASPECTS OF WORSHIP

The Bible offers a great deal of insight about the kinds of activities that facilitate the worship of God. Five aspects of worship emerge from the Scriptures that set a precedent for corporate worship within the church. They are as follows:

1. **Music and Singing** (Exodus 15:1-18; Psalm 92:1, 4; 95:11, 49:1-4; 150:3-5: Matthew 26:30; Acts 2:47; I Corinthians 14:26; Ephesians 5:19)

2. **Proclamation** (1 Chronicles 16:9, 23; Nehemiah 8:1-9; Psalm 95:1; 96:2-3; Hebrews 13:15; 1 Timothy 4:13)

3. **Prayer** (Psalm 66:16-20; Daniel 9:20; Matthew 6:9-13; Acts 4:23-31; Philippians 4:6; 1 Thessalonians 5:17, 25; 1 Timothy 2:1-4)

4. **Giving** (Genesis 14:17-20; 28:22; Leviticus 27:30-33; Numbers 18:21-28; Proverbs 3:9-10; Malachi 3:8-10; Acts 4:34-35; 1 Corinthians 16:1-2)

5. **Observance of ordinances**. It is through the following two ordinances, ordained by Jesus Christ, that we symbolize our commitment to Christ and remember His sacrificial commitment to us:

   • Baptism (Matthew 28:18-20; Acts 2:41; 8:36-39; 10:47-48)

   • The Lord's Supper (Luke 22:14-20; Acts 2:42; 1Corinthians 10:16; 11:17-34)

According to Jesus, what kind of worshippers is His Father seeking (John 4:23-24)? What do you think this means?

EVANGELISM—EXPANDING GOD'S KINGDOM

God intended for the church to be a "going out" people. The Scriptures never present the church as an immobile fellowship, but as an ever-enlarging, always going, unified body of faithful witnesses. This truth certainly influences our role as individual members of the church. The growth and expansion of the Kingdom of God rests largely in our hands. Although God is responsible for building His church (Matthew 16:18), He has appointed us as His disciple-makers (Matthew 28:18-20; Acts 1:8). In fact, the goal of our evangelistic work is to make disciples of Jesus Christ. We are not only seeking a confession of faith in our evangelistic activities, but also a lifelong commitment to the purpose and plan of God for His people, understanding that this is the process through which God builds His church.

What is the central point of Paul's message to the church at Rome concerning evangelism (Romans 10:14)?

What do the following verses reveal about the teaching and preaching ministry of Jesus Christ?

• **Matthew 4:23:**

• **Matthew 9:35:**

• **Mark 1:14-15:**

According to Matthew 24:14, to what extent will the Gospel of the Kingdom be preached before Christ returns for His church?

Jesus wanted all those who followed Him to understand the expectations He had for His disciples. What point was Jesus making in Luke 14:25-33 when He addressed the large crowds that were traveling with Him?

What do the following verses teach about God's desire for all people?

• 1 Timothy 2:3-4:

• 2 Peter 3:9:

Read Matthew 9:36-38 and answer the following questions:

• What was Jesus' response when He saw the crowds of people (verse 36)?

• How were these crowds described (verse 36)?

• How did Jesus describe the harvest (verse 37)? The laborers?

• What did Jesus tell His disciples to do (verse 38)?

• According to verse 38, what activity should precede all others in evangelism?

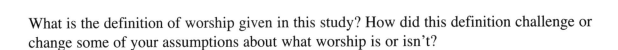

What is the definition of worship given in this study? How did this definition challenge or change some of your assumptions about what worship is or isn't?

Do you agree with the author that the focus of our worship should not be on the forms or the format but on God? Why or why not?

What two essential themes emerge from the Bible in regards to worship? Have you been aware of these two themes during individual and corporate worship times?

From Psalm 96:1-10, make a list of at least 10 things that the Psalmist challenges us to include in our worship of God.

What should the goal of our evangelistic work be? How is the goal hindered when we merely seek a confession of faith and not a lifelong commitment?

Why do you think Jesus Christ left us with the enormous responsibility of disciplemaking? How should this mission affect every area of our lives?

When God's kingdom is expanded through our evangelistic efforts, how is God glorified?

6

WHY DOES THE CHURCH EXIST (PART 3)?

Memory Verse: Ephesians 4:32

FELLOWSHIP—ENCOURAGING GOD'S PEOPLE

Being a disciple of Jesus Christ is never going to be popular with those who do not belong to Him (John 17:14). The world always demands conformity to its values and practices, and they hate anything or anyone that stands opposed to their agenda, especially those who make up the body of Christ. This is exactly why the church must be a place that embraces a culture of encouragement. We desperately need the support of our brothers and sisters in Christ if we are going to take seriously Jesus Christ's command to go out into the world and make disciples. The church is the only place where God's people can gather to find meaningful spiritual relationships and strengthening bonds of mutual support. The truth is we need each other, and Christian fellowship encompasses our responsibilities to encourage one another within the family of God.

Look up each of the following passages and describe our ministry to "one another" within the church:

REFERENCE	RESPONSIBILITY TO "ONE ANOTHER"
Romans 14:19	
Romans 15:7	
Romans 15:14	
Galatians 5:13	
Galatians 6:2	
Ephesians 4:2	
Ephesians 5:21	
Philippians 2:3-4	
Colossians 3:13	
Colossians 3:16	
1 Thessalonians 4:18	
1 Thessalonians 5:11	
Hebrews 10:24-25	
James 5:16	
1 Peter 4:9-10	
1 John 4:7	

MINISTRY—EXTENDING GOD'S GRACE

A great deal of Jesus' earthly ministry was spent healing the sick, helping the poor, and honoring the outcasts (Luke 4:38-41; Matthew 8:14-17; Mark 1:29-34). Everywhere He went He extended His grace to those who needed it most. Jesus' life exemplified the ministry of extending mercy to every facet of human life (Luke 5:27-32; Matthew 9:9-13; Mark 2:13-17). As the body of Jesus Christ, we are to continue His mission today, not only to one another but also to the lost world around us (Galatians 6:10). When we serve unselfishly, in the name of our Savior, endeavoring to meet the physical, emotional, and spiritual needs of those in our church, our community, and our world, we become extensions of our Leader Jesus Christ. Ministering to the needs of others is Kingdom work (Galatians 2:9-10), and this is certainly one of the areas in which our Master was most involved (Luke 4:16-21). Selfless service to a broken and bruised world should characterize the life of every follower of Jesus Christ (Proverbs 31:8-9; Acts 9:36).

What do the following passages reveal about the instructions for ministry that Jesus gave His first disciples on their first short-term mission?

• **Matthew 10:1-16:**

• **Mark 6:7-13:**

• **Luke 9:1-6:**

What is the central point that is being made in the following passages?

• **Matthew 25:34-40:**

• **Matthew 10:40-42:**

• **Hebrews 6:10:**

What does Paul admonish the Galatian Christians to do in Galatians 6:10?

According to 1 Peter 4:10, what are our God-given gifts and abilities to be used for?

What was the one thing that Peter (Cephas), James, and John expected Paul and Barnabas to "remember" as they reached the Gentile world with the Gospel (Galatians 2:9-10)?

What does the writer of Proverbs challenge everyone to do in Proverbs 31:8-9?

DISCUSSION QUESTIONS

SESSION SIX

What should our attitude toward each other be according to Ephesians 4:32? Why is this way of living so counter-culture?

How can the church take seriously its responsibility to be a place of encouragement and support? List some practical ways.

What is the main reason why the church needs to be a place of encouragement? In what other venues is encouragement sought after—although not Christian encouragement?

How would you describe a church that adopted all of Paul's teaching in Ephesians 4:25-32? Would this be the kind of church that you would like to participate in?

Why do you think ministry to the world outside is often overlooked? In what ways is ministry different from evangelism and discipleship? In what ways is it similar?

How can you practice what is preached in Proverbs 31:8-9? What is your reaction to these verses? According to these verses, can ministry to the poor and needy be forgotten?

To what extent do you live out the "religion" described in James 1:27? How do you respond to this biblical description of religion?

HOW IS THE CHURCH SUPPORTED?

Memory Verse: Matthew 6:24

God has always had a plan for supporting the ongoing mission of the local church. Through His providence, He has brought together every necessary ingredient to see the cause of Christ flourish in the villages, cities, and towns all across the world where His people gather. His worldwide plan of reconciliation will not be stopped or hindered because of a resource crisis at the local level. He just wants us to understand our part in this global strategy.

But in order to understand our role in supporting the church, we must turn inward and evaluate how much of what we have has already been surrendered to God, realizing that everything is His anyway (1 Chronicles 29:11, 14; Psalm 50:10; Haggai 2:8). Yes, everything belongs to God! He has simply entrusted us with the responsibility to manage His resources—to properly steward them. (A steward is a person who manages another person's property or possessions.) And He expects that everything we have, not just our money, be used in light of eternity. Because of this, He has not asked us to simply share everything that we have, but to give everything that we have back to Him, understanding the long-term benefits of relinquishment (Luke 14:33; Philippians 3:7-8). God knows that what we grasp too tightly will always hold us back from advancing His kingdom agenda

(Matthew 6:33). And that many times our shortsightedness causes us to look more at the things of the present than on what awaits us in God's eternal kingdom.

According to the following verses, what character traits is God looking for in a steward?

• **Matthew 24:45-51:**

• **Matthew 25:1-13:**

• **Matthew 25:14-30:**

• **Luke 19:11-27:**

BACK TO BASICS

Beginning in Genesis, the Old Testament provides the backdrop for giving to God, instructing God's people to give the first 10% of their income back to Him (Genesis 14:18-20; 28:22). Throughout history, believers have recognized the tithe (or 10% of one's earnings) as the historic benchmark of giving in Scripture (Malachi 3:8-10). Consider the following:

1. Tithing was practiced before the Law was established (Genesis 14:20; 28:22).
2. Tithing was practiced under the Law (Leviticus 27:30; Numbers 18:21-28; Deuteronomy 12:6, 11, 17).
3. Tithing was practiced during Christ's earthly ministry, but not always with the right motives (Matthew 23:23; Luke 11:42; 18:11-14).

Do you think Christians should adopt the biblical benchmark for giving? Why or why not?

During the ministry of Jesus Christ and following the birth of the church at Pentecost, a new standard of giving emerges from within the small but growing fellowship of Christ's followers. The new standard did not eliminate the tithe, but simply raised the bar on sacrificial giving. Giving was now unto Christ, responding to His lavish grace and love. Because of this, the new standard should exceed, and never fall below, the biblical precedent established through tithing.

From the following verses, what patterns of giving emerged within the first century church?

• **Acts 2:44-45:**

• **Acts 4:32-37:**

• **Acts 11:27-30:**

What two areas of giving does God regard as part of our worship?

• **Romans 12:1:**

• **Philippians 4:18-19:**

According to 1 Corinthians 16:1-2, what pattern of giving did the Apostle Paul establish within the churches at Galatia and Corinth?

• **When was the church instructed to give?**

• **Who was instructed to give?**

• How much was to be given?

According to the following verses, who should be remembered when you give?

• Proverbs 19:17:

• 1 Corinthians 9:14 :

• Galatians 6:6:

• James 2:15-16:

What is the sobering reminder Paul gives to Timothy in 1 Timothy 6:7? How should this mindset influence your giving?

What lessons about money and giving are taught in 1 Timothy 6:8-10, 17-19?

SEVEN HABITS OF HIGHLY EFFECTIVE GIVERS

Giving back to God has always been a test of faith and obedience for disciples of Christ. One of the very first areas of your life that God intends to help you gain victory over is in the area of money, possessions, and giving. His Word makes it very clear that you cannot serve both God and money; you will be mastered by one or the other (Matthew 6:24; Luke 16:13). The choice is yours to make. Your full devotion to Christ and His cause will in large part be determined by the habits you develop as a contributor to God's work, because without exception there is nothing that we handle that exposes the condition of our heart like the way we handle our money.

Giving unto God should be done willingly with a heart of joyful worship and anticipation, expecting God to multiply and use the gift for His kingdom's good. There are seven habits of giving that become apparent in Scripture. Consider each one of the following:

1. **Highly effective givers give anonymously** (Matthew 6:3-4). They don't want the attention of the church or its leaders. They give to an audience of One.

2. **Highly effective givers give regularly** (Proverbs 3:9-10; 1 Corinthians 16:2). They are aware that God is the supplier of all of their resources, and they willingly offer the "first-fruits" of all their increase back to God.

3. **Highly effective givers give cheerfully** (2 Corinthians 9:7). They understand that their attitude in giving is more important than the amount of their gift.

4. **Highly effective givers give generously** (2 Corinthians 8:1-7; 9:6). They give above and beyond the expectations of church leaders and out of the overflow of their intense love for God and others.

5. **Highly effective givers give proportionally** (2 Corinthians 8:12; 1 Corinthians 16:1-2). They try to give as much as they are able back to God, recognizing the tithe as the biblical benchmark for giving.

6. **Highly effective givers give locally** (Romans 15:25-29; 1 Corinthians 16:1-2; 2 Corinthians 8:1-3). They gratefully support the local church ministries from which they receive spiritual encouragement, growth, and benefit.

7. **Highly effective givers give expectantly** (2 Corinthians 9:10-15). They don't just offer a donation to an organization. They give an offering unto God, relying on His promise of provision and blessing to far exceed their expectations.

Do you feel satisfied with your current level of giving to God? How will you adjust your giving to reflect the values of a highly effective giver?

How does the Apostle Paul describe the offerings given to God in Philippians 4:18?

What is the promise given to highly effective givers in Proverbs 11:25?

What was the promise Paul made to the Philippian church and to believers everywhere in Philippians 4:19? How can this promise sustain you?

SESSION SEVEN

How is the ongoing mission of the local church supported? What role does God play in this provision?

How would you describe a steward? What responsibilities does a steward have to the owner?

Churches are often criticized for always asking for money. Do you think this would be the case if God's people surrendered to doing their part in supporting the church? Why or why not?

How does Matthew 6:33 compare to the philosophy found on Wall Street or Main Street?

Do you think tithing is a universal principle that applies to all of God's people? Why or why not?

What pattern for giving emerged within the body of Christ following Pentecost? How does this new standard compare to the biblical standard established through tithing?

How is the true condition of our heart exposed through the way that we handle our money?

Why is giving to God an aspect of our worship of Him? When can joyful worship cease and joyless giving begin?

WHAT IS THE CHURCH'S FUTURE?

Memory Verse: 1 Thessalonians 4:16-17

The church should be living in a constant awareness of its future hope. We have not been permanently assigned to this fallen planet. We can eagerly await the advent of our Savior's second coming, a time in which He will call the church, His Bride, unto Himself (1 Thessalonians 4:13-17). Jesus promised His disciples, in no uncertain terms, that He would come again with great power and glory (John 14:3; Mark 13:26), and that the time of His arrival would be when we least expected it (Matthew 24:42, 44; 25:13; Mark 13:32-33). God's Word places the Second Coming of Jesus Christ high on the list of "things to look for." Take a moment to reflect on the following list compiled by Charles Swindoll:

- One out of every 30 verses in the Bible mentions the subject of Christ's return or the end of time.

- Of the 216 chapters in the New Testament, there are well over 300 references to the return of Jesus Christ.

- Only 4 of the 27 New Testament books fail to mention Christ's return.

- That means one-twentieth of the entire New Testament is dedicated to the subject of our Lord's return.

- In the Old Testament, such well-known and reliable men of God as Job, Moses, David, Isaiah, Jeremiah, Daniel, and most of the minor prophets, fixed at least part of their attention on the Lord's return.

- Christ spoke of His return often, especially after He had revealed His death. He never did so in vague or uncertain terms.

- Those who lived on following His teaching, who established the churches and wrote the Scriptures in the first century, frequently mentioned His return in their preaching and in their writings.[3]

Wow! One-twentieth of the New Testament talks about the return of our Lord. Certainly we should be anticipating that glorious day when we will meet the Lord in the air. If the inspired Word of God places such emphasis on the Second Coming, we should take notice and watch for that wonderful rapture of the church as well.

What is the main lesson being taught in the following verses?

• **1 Corinthians 1:7:**

• **Philippians 3:20:**

• **Philippians 4:5:**

• **1 Thessalonians 1:10:**

• **1 Thessalonians 5:6:**

What promise did Jesus make in Revelation 22:20? How did John respond to Christ's promised return?

According to the following verses, what are the patterns of living that should characterize those who are awaiting Christ's return?

• **Luke 12:37:**

• **1 Corinthians 15:58:**

• **1 John 3:2-3:**

WHAT TO EXPECT

What will eternity with Jesus Christ be like? Scholars, theologians, pastors, and students have all passionately discussed the state of the church following the Second Coming of Jesus Christ. There are certain things we do know, because they are revealed in Scripture. We certainly can know what to expect at the appearing of our Lord and Savior, thanks to the Apostle Paul. We can also begin to develop an idea of what our glorified bodies will be like, what heaven will be like, and what life will be like.

From 1 Thessalonians 4:13-18, list in order the events that will take place when Jesus Christ returns for His church.

How does the Apostle Paul compare and contrast our physical bodies with our resurrection bodies in 1 Corinthians 15:42-55?

PHYSICAL BODIES	RESURRECTION BODIES

What promise does Paul give us regarding our resurrection bodies in 1 Corinthians 15:49 (1 John 3:2)? What are some of the qualities of our resurrection body that are revealed in John 20:19, 26?

How is the "New Jerusalem" described in the following verses?

REFERENCE	DESCRIPTION
• Revelation 21:3	
• Revelation 21:4	
• Revelation 21:22	
• Revelation 21:23	
• Revelation 21:25	
• Revelation 21:27	
• Revelation 22:3	
• Revelation 22:5	

Heaven will be beyond our human comprehension. The eternal state of those who are God's will endure forever, and God Himself will dwell in the midst of His perfect people, as He originally intended at the beginning of time. Imagine a place where no death exists and where your occupation will be to worship God and enjoy Him forever. How can words begin to describe the future state of the church of Jesus Christ? We have a glorious hope that defies all imagination.

IN THE MEANTIME

Until Jesus Christ does return for His church, we are given very specific instructions in Scripture to continue Jesus' mission. Certainly predicting the date of His arrival is impossible in light of Jesus own words to His disciples. So what should Christians do in the meantime? Since we don't know the day or the hour, what decade or even what century He will return, what are we supposed to be doing before Christ comes?

1. We must continue to worship God individually and corporately (John 4:23).
2. We must continue to fellowship with God's people (Hebrews 10:24-25).
3. We must continue to make disciples (Matthew 28:18-20).
4. We must continue to pray for His return (Ephesians 6:18)
5. We must continue to study His Word (2 Timothy 2:15; 1 Peter 2:2).
6. We must continue to extend God's grace to others (1 John 3:17-18).
7. We must continue to be Christ's church (Ephesians 5:27).

What changes are you inspired to make in your life as a result of studying the Second Coming of Christ?

DISCUSSION QUESTIONS

SESSION EIGHT

What process is the church currently undergoing in preparation for the Second Coming of Jesus Christ (Ephesians 4:25-27)?

Who is the only person who knows when Christ will return for His church (Mark 13:32)? Why do you think that so many second coming prophesies regarding the day and date of Christ's return have been made?

Who does Jesus describe Himself as in Mark 13:35? What is our responsibility include while we wait for His return (Mark 13:34)?

Why do you think the Bible places such an emphasis on the Second Coming of Christ? Does it serve as both a reminder to the saved and a warning to the lost? How?

How would you describe eternity with God? Can Heaven be fully understood by our finite minds?

What kind of emotions bubble up when you hear someone talking about the Second Coming? Are you excited? Fearful? Uncertain?

If you were to spend a few moments with Jesus, and you could ask Him about His upcoming return, what questions would you ask Him? Do you think His answers would change the way you live right now?

[1] William Barclay, *New Testament Words* (Louisville, Kentucky: Westminster John Knox Press, 1974), p. 70.

[2] Ralph Martin, *The Worship of God* (Grand Rapids, Michigan: Eerdmans, 1982), p. 4.

[3] Charles R. Swindoll, *Growing Deep In The Christian Life* (Portland, Oregon: Multnomah Press, 1986), p. 268.

JOURNEY INTO THE HEART OF AUTHENTIC DISCIPLESHIP

THE DISCIPLESHIP

CHALLENGE

APPENDIXES

DISCIPLESHIP INVENTORY—Read each item, and using a pencil, check the box that best represents an accurate, personal evaluation.

	Always	Usually	Sometimes	Seldom	Never
DAILY INTERACTION WITH GOD:					
I have a daily time to spend with God.	❏	❏	❏	❏	❏
I recognize Jesus as the Leader of my life.	❏	❏	❏	❏	❏
I sense God's presence throughout the day.	❏	❏	❏	❏	❏
I try to keep myself spiritually disciplined.	❏	❏	❏	❏	❏
I know that God disciplines me.	❏	❏	❏	❏	❏
I read my Bible every day.	❏	❏	❏	❏	❏
I study my Bible at least once each week.	❏	❏	❏	❏	❏
I memorize Scripture on a weekly basis.	❏	❏	❏	❏	❏
I pray for the needs and concerns of others.	❏	❏	❏	❏	❏
I have a prayer list that I regularly refer to.	❏	❏	❏	❏	❏
My daily prayers include adoration, thanksgiving, confession, and supplication.	❏	❏	❏	❏	❏
I journal what God has revealed to me through His Word, prayer, His Spirit, and His people in order to apply it to my life.	❏	❏	❏	❏	❏
DIRECT INVOLVEMENT IN THE LOCAL CHURCH:					
I desire to live in unity with others in my church.	❏	❏	❏	❏	❏
I seek to resolve all disputes and arguments that I have with other Christians or that they have with me.	❏	❏	❏	❏	❏
I genuinely love God's people.	❏	❏	❏	❏	❏
I live in harmony with members of my spiritual family.	❏	❏	❏	❏	❏
I serve God by serving in my church.	❏	❏	❏	❏	❏
I willingly give at least 10% of my income back to God through my local church.	❏	❏	❏	❏	❏
I involve myself in regular acts of kindness to those in need.	❏	❏	❏	❏	❏
DELIBERATE INVESTMENT IN THE GREAT COMMISSION:					
I pray daily for the salvation of lost people.	❏	❏	❏	❏	❏
I share my personal testimony with nonbelievers when the opportunity arises.	❏	❏	❏	❏	❏
I share the Good News with those who are receptive.	❏	❏	❏	❏	❏
I look for opportunities every day to point people to Jesus Christ.	❏	❏	❏	❏	❏
I eagerly pursue disciplemaking relationships with new believers.	❏	❏	❏	❏	❏
I always have my kingdom mission clearly in mind.	❏	❏	❏	❏	❏

Subtotals: ___ ___ ___ ___ ___

x4 x3 x2 x1

Totals: ___ ___ ___ ___ ___

Overall Score: _____

Scoring:

To calculate your discipleship inventory score, add each column except the "Never" column. Each item checked in the "Always" column is worth four points; the "Usually" column, three points; the "Sometimes" column, two points; the "Seldom" column, one point. Add your four totals together to get your overall score out of a possible one hundred.

What Does Your Score Mean?

While we hope that the Discipleship inventory is a helpful tool for you, remember that your score is a general benchmark, not a foolproof diagnostic indicator. Keep this in mind as you consider what the inventory may mean for you.

For Further Thought:

Do you feel that your score accurately reflects your life of discipleship? Why or why not?

What are some other aspects of discipleship that should be taken into account but are not included in the Discipleship Inventory?

On a scale of 1 to 10, how would you evaluate your current discipleship? How did you come up with that number?

Ask your discipler or another Christian who knows you well, how he would evaluate your life of discipleship. Look for specific areas of your life that you need to improve or strengthen. Write these "improvement areas" below.

DAILY IN THE WORD

Daily in the Word is a very practical spiritual growth discipline that will assist you in deepening your relationship with God through His Word. It consists of five very simple steps. Each of the following steps should be completed daily:

Step #1: Write the day and date on the page of a notebook or notepad.

Step #2: Write out a verse or series of verses that spoke to you during your Bible reading.

Step #3: Answer one or more of the following questions in your notebook:

- What sin should I avoid?
- What promise can I lean on?
- What command should I obey?
- What blessing can I enjoy?
- What lesson can I learn from?
- What victory has been promised?
- What aspect of God, Jesus, or the Holy Spirit was revealed?
- What attitude should I change?
- What path should I follow?
- What person should I speak to?

Step #4: Write out a prayer of commitment that reveals your response to the things the Lord has taught you.

- What does God want me to do?
- How should this passage change the way I think or live?
- How does this passage change my attitude?

Step #5: Exchange your spiritual journal with another Christ follower.

See the next page for an example of a Daily In The Word journal entry.

DAILY IN THE WORD JOURNAL ENTRY

DAY AND DATE: Thursday, July 8

VERSE: Psalm 119:2 *"Blessed are they that keep his testimonies, and that seek him with the whole heart."*

QUESTION: What blessing can I enjoy?

God is graciously offering me an opportunity to be blessed—to be happy and content in my relationship with Him. But in order to receive the full measure of His blessing, I must commit myself to two things. First, I am to keep His testimonies. Second, God desires that I seek Him with my whole heart. I realize that these two things are accomplished through daily interaction with God in His Word and prayer.

PRAYER: Father, You have once again revealed Your truth to me through Your Word. Thank you for allowing Your Holy Spirit to illuminate the pages of Scripture. I eagerly desire Your blessing. I want to find all surpassing joy and contentment in my relationship with You. Enable me to keep your testimonies and seek You with every ounce of my being. Please help me to cross paths with someone today who needs to be in a relationship with You. Amen.